Baby & Toddler Play Book

This wonderful compendium of joyful playthings, books and music will take you every step of the way through a baby's first three years! Nor have the authors forgotten to include those special person-to-person games that little children love. This collection helps adults make wise choices for the youngest children.

—*Nancy Balaban, Ed.D.*
Infant and Parent Development
and Early Intervention Program,
Bank Street Graduate School of Education

The Oppenheims have interspersed sound development information with games and toys to enhance burgeoning skills. Lucky is the child whose parent uses this book for all its wisdom and wonder!

—*Susan Strecker Richard, Editor-in-Chief*
Lamaze Family Magazine

Oppenheim Toy Portfolio Baby & Toddler Play Book is filled with playful games to teach and entertain your little one.

—*Working Mother Magazine*

OPPENHEIM TOY PORTFOLIO

Baby & Toddler Play Book

Joanne Oppenheim
and **Stephanie Oppenheim**

Illustrations by **Joan Auclair**

With thanks to our family and the many other families who helped us test for the best.

—Joanne & Stephanie

This book may be purchased for educational, business, or sales promotional use. For information contact: Stephanie Oppenheim, Publisher, Oppenheim Toy Portfolio, Inc., 40 East 9th St., Suite 14M, New York NY 10003 or call (212) 598-0502 or e-mail stephanie@toyportfolio.com.

Designed by Joan Auclair
Jacket design by James Oppenheim

ISBN: 0-9664823-3-6

Contents

Introduction

Playing with your baby is more than fun—play is key to learning. But knowing what games to play or what toys to buy is confusing. Unfortunately, new babies arrive without instructions. Finally, here is the instruction manual for play! From patty-cake to teddy bears, it tells you everything you need to know about toys and play from day one to their third birthday!

These first three years have a tremendous impact on your child's development. Experts agree that babies who are engaged, nurtured, and stimulated become better learners. This book is designed to help you know what to do to make the most of this all-important time in your child's life.

No other period in life is marked with such amazing physical, intellectual, and social growth as these first exciting years. In just a matter of weeks babies go from merely gazing at things to reaching out to explore. In a matter of months they go from sitting up with help to crawling, standing upright, and even taking their first independent steps. In less than a year they go from babbling to understanding and making themselves understood. During these three short years they grow from being your baby to being your big boy or big girl.

As babies develop they need playthings and people to play games that match their ever-changing abilities. Unlike stretch socks, few toys are designed so that one size fits all. Just like the clothes they keep outgrowing, playthings for babies and toddlers need to "fit." Knowing what games to play and what toys to choose can enhance each developmental milestone—building your child's sense of "can-do."

But choosing the right toys can be confusing. Not only do babies arrive without play instructions, many of us don't live close enough to grandparents or experienced aunts and uncles who used to show new parents the tricks of the trade. New parents often feel clueless. There are so many choices out there it's hard to know what to bring home. Nor do we know instinctively what games to play with a tiny baby.

That's what this book is all about. It's a guide for having fun with your child—a resource for age-appropriate toys plus a collection of games that you can play with your baby and toddler. Isn't it wonderful that something that's as much fun as play is also good for them!

What Babies & Toddlers Learn From Play

Learning through play is not about teaching babies to walk or talk sooner. It's not about training toddlers to read and count before they are steady on their feet. Just consider the many ways children learn through their play:

- **Big Muscles & Coordination.** It's through active play that little ones develop big muscles and coordination that allow them to crawl, stand, toddle, walk, run, jump, and climb.
- **Fine Motor Skills.** Play provides the motivation and practice to gain control of the little muscles of their hands and fingers with ever-growing precision. Baby's accidental swipes at things gradually grow into more purposeful reaching out, grasping, and exploration. As their fine motor skills grow, children discover the wonderful power of making things happen.
- **Social Development.** Babies are by nature social beings, and the give and take of playful games of patty-cake, roly-poly ball, and other playful interactions, foster baby's positive feelings about themselves and others.
- **Language & Imagination.** Play fosters the growth of language and the ability to communicate. As language grows so does the imagination and the ability to pretend.

- **Intellectual Growth.** Through play babies develop early thinking, memory, and problem-solving skills. For example, in playing little games of peek-a-boo baby gradually learns that out of sight does not mean gone and forgotten.
- **Fun & Refreshment.** For both parents and children, and throughout life, play is an important way to recharge one's batteries and release stress. Unlike work which must be done, play is a voluntary activity.

What's all the talk about synapses?

Recent studies about brain development reinforce the importance of providing infants and toddlers with a stimulating environment. Put simply, the brain is not completely hardwired at birth. Synapses, or connections, continue to be made. The best ways to foster such development is by providing a rich interactive environment—and by that we mean interactions of the human kind. Talking, singing, holding, playing games, and introducing appropriate playthings all have a positive cumulative effect that helps your baby's intellectual as well as social and emotional development.

Misconceptions about Smart Toys

There's a lot of hype directed at parents about bringing home smart toys—toys that start drilling tots with the ABCs and 1-2-3s before they can even talk! If your instincts told you that this was not an important piece of business for your baby and toddler, you were absolutely right.

Truly smart toys for babies and toddlers are those that stimulate your child's natural curiosity and invite exploration. Many of the shape sorters, stackers, and other quiz machines directed to very young children are anything but smart. Many operate on the premise that learning can be reduced to a series of right and wrong answers and that sooner is better than later.

Pushing early academics can be done, but often the same skills are learned more quickly and with greater ease later. Rushing tots to get on the smart track can seriously derail learning and positive attitudes about learning and themselves as learners. Ultimately, if they emerge from baby- and toddlerhood as confident doers, the stage is set for a lifetime of positive learning experiences. It's not that you shouldn't count with your toddler, but she doesn't need formal lessons—and other things count, too.

How We Select the Best

Here at the Oppenheim Toy Portfolio, we shop for children year-round—only we get to do what most parents wish they could do before they buy. We open the toys, run the videos, read the books, play the music, and boot up the software. We get to compare all the toys that may look remarkably similar but often turn out to be quite different. For example, we put the toy trains together and find out which ones don't stay on the tracks.

How We're Different

The Oppenheim Toy Portfolio was founded in 1989 as the only independent consumer review of children's media. Unlike most other groups that rate products, we do not charge entry fees or accept ads from manufacturers. When you see our award seals on products, you can be assured that they are "award-winning" because they were selected with a focus on children's developmental interests and skills, and then rated by the most objective panel of judges—kids.

The Real Experts Speak: Kids and Their Families

To get a meaningful sampling, we deal with families from all walks of life. We have testers in the city and in the country, in diapers and in blue jeans, in school clothes and in tutus. They have parents who are teachers, secretaries, lawyers, doctors, writers, engineers, doormen, software programmers, editors, psychologists, librarians, engineers, business people, architects, family therapists, musicians, artists, nurses, and early childhood educators. In some instances we have tested products in preschool and after-school settings where we can get feedback from groups of children. Since all new products tend to have novelty appeal, we ask our testers to live with a product for a while before assessing it. Among other things, we always ask—would you recommend it to others?

Criteria We Use for Choosing Quality Products

- What is this product designed to do and how well does it do it?
- What can the child do with the product? Does it invite active doing and thinking or simply passive watching?
- Is it safe and well-designed, and can it withstand the unexpected?
- Does it "fit" the developmental needs, interests, and typical skills of the children for whom it was designed?
- What message does it convey? Toys as well as books and videos can say a great deal about values parents are trying to convey. For example, does the product reflect old sexual stereotypes that limit children's views of themselves and others?
- What will a child learn from this product? Is it a "smart" product that will engage the child's mind or simply a novelty with limited play value?
- Is it entertaining? No product makes our list if kids find it boring, no matter how "good" or "educational" it claims to be.
- Is the age label correct? Is the product so easy that it will be boring or so challenging that it will be frustrating?

Rating System

Outstanding products are awarded one of four honors:

Platinum Award—These represent the most innovative, engaging new products of the year.

Gold Seal Award—Given to outstanding new products that enhance the lives of children. All products selected for this book have received a Gold Seal Award unless they are marked Platinum Award or Blue Chip. Those products that receive a Gold Seal during the year are nominated for the year-end top Platinum Award List.

Blue Chip Classic Award—Reserved for classic products that should not be missed just because they weren't invented yesterday.

SNAP Award—Our Special Needs Adaptable Product Award is given to products that can be used by or easily adapted for children with special needs. The reviews of the SNAP Award winners are found in our annual book.

Our annual book, *Oppenheim Toy Portfolio: The Best Toys, Books, Videos, Music & Software For Kids*, includes reviews for products for children from infancy through age 10.

Using This Book

Each section begins with a play profile that tells you what to expect during each developmental stage and what "basic gear" will enhance learning and play. We also give you suggestions for best gifts for your budget and, perhaps most importantly, a stage-by-stage list of toys to avoid.

Because we know how busy people are these days, our reviews are purposely short and provide information on how to get your hands on the product.

A word about prices: Our award-winning products are not all high-ticket items. We have selected the very best products in toy supermarkets, as well as those that you will find in specialty stores, museum shops, and quality catalogs. We have listed the suggested retail prices, but they will vary tremendously depending on where you shop.

Telephone numbers: Where available, we have given a customer service number in case you have difficulty locating the product in your area.

Timing is Everything & Know Thy Baby

Knowing *when* to play can be as important as knowing *what* to play. The trick is in tuning in for those playful moments when your baby can be engaged. A toddler who is hungry or overtired is in no mood for play. Trust yourself—reading your child's body language means knowing when to step back or change what you are doing, or when baby wants more, more, more.

All babies do not respond in the same way to the same games and playthings. Babies come to us with different temperaments. Some are more laid back than others. For example, some toddlers brighten up when they hear lively music; others become fretful or cover their ears. Your baby may be reduced to giggles when you "fly" him overhead, or such vigorous play may reduce him to tears and fears. Respecting their likes and dislikes and anticipating their responses will make for a happier child.

Happy Playing!

Joanne Stephanie

I • Toys

1 • Infants
Birth to One Year

What to Expect Developmentally

The Horizontal Infant

Your Role in Play. To your newborn, no toy in the world is more interesting than you! Babies are more interested in people than things. Your smiling face, your gentle touch, the sound of your voice, even your familiar scent make you the most perfect plaything. Don't worry about spoiling your newborn with attention. Responding to your baby's needs now will make him less needy later. Playing with your baby is not just fun—it's one of the most important ways babies learn about themselves and the world of people and things!

Learning Through the Senses. Right from the start, babies begin learning by looking, listening, touching, smelling, and tasting. It's through their senses that they make sense of the world. In this first remarkable year, babies progress from gazing to grasping, from touching to tossing, from watching to doing. By selecting a rich variety of playthings, parents can match their baby's sensory learning style.

Reaching Out. Initially, you will be the one to activate the mobile, shake the rattle, squeeze the squeaker. But before long, baby will be reaching out and taking hold of things and engaging you in a game of peek-a-boo.

Toys and Development. As babies develop, so do their needs for playthings that fit their growing abilities. Like clothes, good toys need to fit. Some of the toys for newborns will have short-term use and then get packed away or passed along to a new cousin or friend. Others will be used in new ways as your child grows. During this first year, babies need toys to gaze at, listen to, grasp, chomp on, shake, pass from one hand to another, bang together, toss, chase, and hug.

Time was when infants' rooms and products were all pastel. Not any more—research has shown that during the early weeks of life babies respond to the sharp contrast of black-and-white patterns. But does that mean your whole nursery needs to be black and white? Not at all. In no time, your baby is going to be responding to bright colors, interesting sounds, and motion.

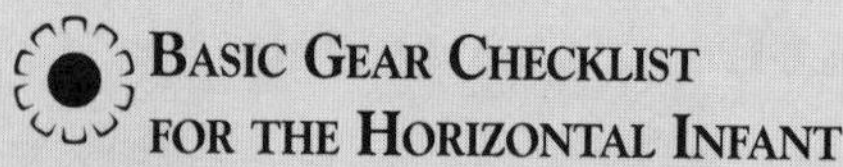

Basic Gear Checklist for the Horizontal Infant

- ✓ **Mobile**
- ✓ **Musical toys**
- ✓ **Crib mirror**
- ✓ **Soft fabric toys with differing sounds and textures**
- ✓ **Fabric dolls or animals with easy-to-grab limbs**
- ✓ **Activity mat**

Toys to Avoid

These toys pose choking and/or suffocation hazards:

- ✓ **Antique rattles**
- ✓ **Foam toys**
- ✓ **Toys with elastic**
- ✓ **Toys with buttons, bells, and ribbons**
- ✓ **Old wooden toys that may contain lead paint**
- ✓ **Furry plush dolls that shed**
- ✓ **Any toys with small parts**

Crib Toys

Musical Toys, Mobiles, and Mirrors

Few toys are as soothing to newborns as a music box with its quiet sounds. Today, most musical toys for infants don't come as boxes but as plush toys. We prefer some of the newer pull-down musical toys to soft plush dolls with hard metal wind-up keys that older babies may chew or get poked with by accident. When baby starts turning over, use musical wind-up plush dolls with supervision, not as crib toys.

■ **Flatso Farm Musical Pulldown**

(North American Bear $36) Framed in a soft red barn, sheep, duck, and cow watch a wiggly piglet ride up to the tune of "Old MacDonald." PLATINUM AWARD '99. Bring home with soft velour **Flatso Rattles** ($10), with eye-catching patterned bodies and gentle sounds. This company's PLATINUM AWARD-winning **Crib Notes Watering Can** ($36), with a friendly spider hanging down from the green and pink velour watering can, plays "Eensy Weensy Spider." (800) 682-3427.

■ **Enchanted Garden Sunflower Pull Musical**

(Manhattan Toy $20) Attach this smiley yellow sunflower to baby's crib. A perky blue and yellow bug rides the long green stem inching up as it plays "Beautiful Dreamer." PLATINUM AWARD '97. (800) 747-2454.

◆◆◆◆◆◆◆◆◆◆◆◆◆◆◆◆◆◆◆◆◆◆◆◆

SMART PARENT TRICK

Slow'n'Easy. Put toys in baby's sight line, but allow time for baby to reach out and take hold of objects visually and later with her hands. Just as you pause to let baby respond to your voice with her own sounds, you need to give baby time to reach out and take hold of things. This is not an instantaneous skill. Motivate baby to reach out and swipe at, toys attached to crib rail with Velcro, or toys that you hold for her. Choose objects that are soft and easy to grasp.

■ Enchanted Garden Mini-Mobile

(Manhattan Toy $20) Attach this brightly colored ring with a sunflower on top and three little friendly bugs hanging from the bottom to the stroller or crib. A brightly colored toy like this one will motivate baby to reach out and touch. With stitched features, this is a totally safe early gazing and reaching out toy. (800) 747-2454.

■ Slumbertime Soother

(Fisher-Price $34.99) Everyone's been there—the baby is almost asleep but the music has stopped. If you walk into the room to turn it back on, you start the whole process over again. To the rescue—an innovative remote-controlled musical toy that can be restarted from 20 feet. Has lights that change with the music, or nature sounds. Plays 10 lullabies that can be adjusted for volume (a plus). Takes 4 C and 2 AA batteries. PLATINUM AWARD '99. (800) 435-5437.

■ Action Musical Peter Rabbit

(Eden $23) There are a lot of Peter Rabbit products for babies. This cheery 10" velour version of Peter moves his head as the music plays. We also recommend the BLUE CHIP **Peter Rabbit Musical Pillow** (Eden $20), an 8" embroidered pillow that is ideal for tying onto a newborn's bassinet, crib, or stroller. A small comforting take-along for trips away from home. (800) 443-4275.

■ Lights 'n' Sound Aquarium

(Fisher-Price $29.99) Attach this innovative toy to the crib rail for your infant's listening and gazing pleasure. Two little fish swim about in a "aquarium" and you can choose either music box tunes or sounds of the sea. Another setting projects "waves" on the ceiling. Happily there's a volume control. Looked promising, but was not ready for testing. Takes 4 "C"batteries. (800) 432-5437.

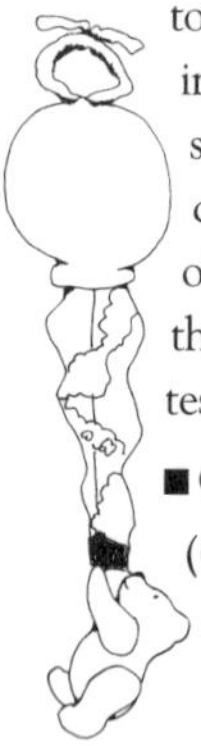

■ Classical Pooh Pullstring Musical

(Gund $25) This PLATINUM AWARD-winning Pooh is holding onto a red balloon—in search of honey, of course! (732) 248-1500.

SMART PARENT TRICK

You heard that babies need stimulation, so you figure you should put tons of toys (1) in the crib, (2) on the walls, (3) in the stroller. The truth is, babies stop looking at things that are always there, just as you stop looking at a vase that's always in the same place. Changing things to gaze at will interest babies more. Also, it's hard to focus on too many objects at once. So less may be more.

BABY TALK GAMES

You Don't Say! Some new parents feel awkward about speaking to a baby who can't yet talk. What can you talk about? Anything. The words aren't important. Talk about what you are doing, even if you are changing a diaper. Imitate baby's coos, gurgles, squeaks and squeals. In the beginning you'll do most of the talking . . . but before long baby will be answering with gurgles and goos. Be sure to pause so baby can take turns—before long you'll be having real "chats."

Monkey See, Monkey Do. Long before they can talk with words, babies will respond if you engage them in "conversations." Copy the faces your baby makes. If baby sticks out her tongue, you do it too. If baby sneezes, you sneeze; if she hiccups, hiccup back. Who says you need words to "talk"?

Mobiles

A musical mobile attached to crib rail or changing table provides baby with fascinating sights and sounds. During the first three months, infants can focus only on objects that are relatively close. Toys should be between 8" and 14" from their eyes. Before you buy any mobile, look at it from the baby's perspective. What can you see? Many attractive mobiles are purely for decoration and do not have images that face the baby in the crib. Here are our favorites:

■ Sensational Circus Musical Mobile

(Manhattan Toy $40) Baby can watch these bright eye-grabbers as they spin. Newest from an appealing series of mobiles with different themes. Also recommended, **Merry Meadows** (Platinum Award '98) or the **Enchanted Garden Mobile.** Designed from the horizontal baby's perspective with faces smiling down at baby. All play Brahms' "Lullabye." (800) 747-2454.

■ Flatso Farm Mobile

(North American Bear $54) A companion piece to the **Flatso Farm Musical Pulldown,** this charming mobile has a cow, duck, pig, and lamb dangling from a red barn. Plays "Farmer in the Dell." Also very special, **Baby Bed Bugs Mobile.** (800) 682-3427.

■ Wimmer-Ferguson Infant Stim-Mobile Blue Chip

(Manhattan Toy $20) Newborns will be fascinated with the black-and-white, high-contrast patterns of the ten vinyl 3" discs and squares that dance and dangle on this nonmusical mobile for the crib or changing table. May not look as cute as other mobiles, but babies do react to the visual stimulation of this early crib toy. (800) 747-2454.

■ Sesame Street Musical Mobile

(Tyco Preschool $24.99) Elmo, Ernie, Cookie, and Big Bird all move to the tune of "Sunny Day." The characters are looking down at your baby. Most mobiles we found this year do not. Pass on mobiles that are so pale and bland that there is nothing for the baby to look at except the motion. (800) 367-8926.

SAFETY TIP: Mobiles should be removed by the time baby is five months, or whenever she can reach out and touch them, to avoid the danger of strangulation or choking on small parts.

Crib Mirrors

Even before he can reach out and touch, a crib mirror provides your baby ever-changing images. It will be a while before baby knows whose face and hands he sees. In time, he'll be babbling to that face and studying the reflection of his hands.

■ Wimmer-Ferguson Double-Feature Crib Mirror Blue Chip

(Manhattan Toy $34) A truly distortion-free crib mirror. Comes with mirror on one side and high-contrast graphics, including a face and a boat, on the other side; the latter will be of greatest interest to younger babies. Unlike many crib toys, this mirror ties at all four corners, so it can't be used as a lift-and-bang toy like many other crib mirrors. (800) 747-2454.

■ Glow-in-the-Dark Crib Mirror

(Infantino $15) Framed in soft fabric this 10" x 14" infant-safe mirror is distortion-free and ties on to the crib rail. Choose yellow or blue; the oblong mirror has glow-in-the-dark stars and dots—a nice touch when it's time for lights out. (800) 365-8182.

SAFETY TIP: Many catalogs and picturebooks show baby cribs overflowing with quilts, pillows, and toys. These are pretty to look at, but totally unsafe! See safety check list for cribs (pg. 139).

SMART PARENT TRICK

New parents often try to comfort a crying baby by bouncing her gently in their arms. Many babies will in fact stop crying if you stop bouncing. Ask yourself, when you have gas, do you really want someone to bounce you? Try holding your baby close and gently pat her back or rock her as you sing quietly. Babies under a month old are also comforted from their own movements by being swaddled.

◆◆◆◆◆◆◆◆◆◆◆◆◆◆◆◆◆◆◆◆◆◆◆◆◆◆◆◆◆◆◆

BABY TRACKING GAMES

Following a moving object is no small feat for the new baby. Use a boldly patterned soft toy with quiet rattle or squeaky sound to get baby's attention. Give it a shake and move it slowly from side to side in baby's line of vision. In time baby will reach out to touch, but for now looking and listening is the name of the game. Remember, newborns can't focus on objects more than 8–14 inches from their eyes.

Everything That Goes Up Here's a little baby science lesson. Hold your hand up in the air in baby's sight line saying:
"Everything that goes up comes down, down, down!"
(Gradually spiral your hand down, down, down 'til you gently tickle baby under the chin or on the tummy.) Before long baby will anticipate the tickles and giggle before your fingers touch!

Buzzing Bees Babies love the surprise action and sound of this little hand game that involves listening, watching, and feeling.

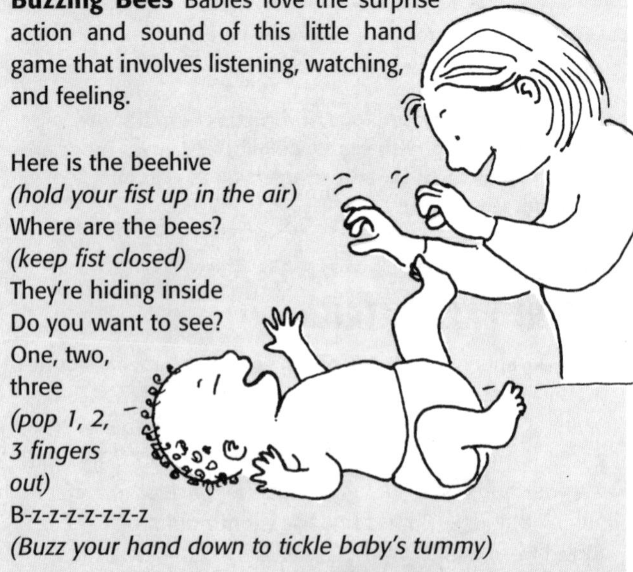

Here is the beehive
(hold your fist up in the air)
Where are the bees?
(keep fist closed)
They're hiding inside
Do you want to see?
One, two,
three
*(pop 1, 2,
3 fingers
out)*
B-z-z-z-z-z-z-z
(Buzz your hand down to tickle baby's tummy)

◆◆◆◆◆◆◆◆◆◆◆◆◆◆◆◆◆◆◆◆◆◆◆◆◆◆◆◆

Equipment for Playtime

Babies are such social beings that they are happiest when they are in the midst of the action. While many of these products have a short lifespan, they serve an important function by providing a special place for viewing the world.

■ **Funtime Soft Bouncer Seat** BLUE CHIP

(Summer Infant $50) This fabric chair provides the perfect perspective for young infants who are ready for a little elevation but are not able to sit up. Comes with spinning toys on a bar that baby will first gaze at and later activate. Use with adult supervision only. Up to 25 pounds. (800) 268-6237.

SAFETY TIP: Never place any type of baby carrier on a table, bed, or counter. Even though the baby has never done it before, there's no way of predicting when he will make a move that can tip the carrier.

SMART PARENT TRICK

Puff'n'Pop. Puff your cheeks. Then use your hands to pop them as you pop them to make a funny noise. Soon, baby will reach out to pop your cheeks for you.

Zerberts. Use any excuse to give your baby a wet zerbert kiss. Puff your lips and let it rip!

Playmats

There are lots of good choices here at all prices. As a general rule avoid playmats and blankets that have lots of doodads that pose a choking hazard. We found many expensive quilts with ribbons, buttons, and fuzzy trims that are unsafe. Also avoid mats with activities all over and no really comfortable place for baby to lie down. Here are our favorites:

■ Enchanted Garden Playmat

(Manhattan Toy $60) This new colorful mat has yellow flowers on a red field with blue and white polka dotted "bumper" ring around it. There's a flower mirror, a sunflower that turns with a ratchet sound, a textured caterpillar to feel, a peek-a-boo ladybug, and a teether that tucks away. These sensory items make for an interesting environment even before baby has much mobility. (800) 747-2454.

■ Deluxe Gymini 3-D Activity Gym BLUE CHIP

(Tiny Loves $39.95–50) Gyms with dangly toys to swipe at are enjoyed for a short period of time. This soft version, a play mat with two arches, got high marks for keeping baby entertained. Also available in high-contrast black, white, and red version. Not for babies who are beginning to pull themselves up. New deluxe version is slightly larger. (800) 843-6292. We much prefer this product to traditional plastic activity gyms that have gotten mixed reports. Older babies have gotten feet caught and even kicked a few over. Our caution remains with any gym you use—total supervision is required.

SAFETY TIP: Many parents find the back-and-forth action of a swing a soothing diversion for a restless infant. However, we find it difficult to recommend any infant swings because they can entrap limbs and necks or even collapse. If you choose to use one, we urge you not to leave the room. Use it with constant supervision.

SMART BABY TRICK

By 2–2½ months, when baby opens his little fists, try putting a soft rattle in his hand. He may not hold it for long, but the feel and sound of a soft rattle will help him notice his hands and how they move. Discovering his hands and how he can bring them together, pull them apart, move them in and out of sight will be more amazing than any toy for now. You don't need to attach toys to his hands and feet. In fact, many babies dislike the distraction.

First Lap and Floor Toys:
Rattles, Sound Toys, and More

Infant toys can help adults engage and interact with newborns. A bright rattle that baby tracks visually, a quiet music box that soothes, or an interesting doll to gaze or swipe at are ideal for beginning getting-acquainted games. These toys can be used at the changing table or for lap games during playful moments after a feeding, before a bath, or whenever.

■ Lamaze First Mirror

(Learning Curve $19.99) A fabric-covered wedge with a mirror for baby to peer into, covered in eye-grabbing bold black & white patterns with red piping. The mirror in a soft fabric frame can be removed and used separately. PLATINUM AWARD '98. (800) 704-8697.

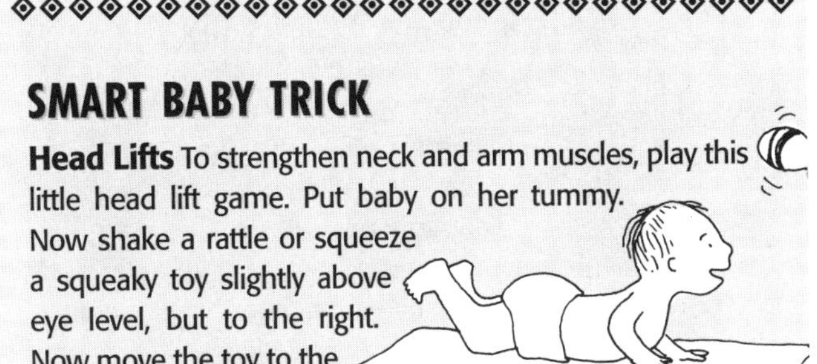

◈◈◈◈◈◈◈◈◈◈◈◈◈◈◈◈◈◈◈◈◈◈◈◈◈◈◈◈◈◈◈

SMART BABY TRICK

Head Lifts To strengthen neck and arm muscles, play this little head lift game. Put baby on her tummy. Now shake a rattle or squeeze a squeaky toy slightly above eye level, but to the right. Now move the toy to the left and back again.

◈◈◈◈◈◈◈◈◈◈◈◈◈◈◈◈◈◈◈◈◈◈◈◈◈◈◈◈◈◈◈

■ Tolo Gramophone Music Box

(Small World $20) Wind the knob and a teddy bear cranks the roller wheel as the music plays. An old-fashioned gramophone horn ratchets when turned; there are beads to finger and a small mirror for peeking into. (800) 421-4153.

■ Tolo Safety Mirror & Rattle Set

(Small World $12) Here's a combo baby gift with hours of play value. There's a blue man-in-the-moon teething ring rattle with three star clackers that are soft enough to chomp on packaged with a hand-held mirror/rattle that is framed with the man-in-the moon and reverses to a smiling yellow sun. (800) 421-4153.

■ Lamaze Peek-a-boo Puppet

(Learning Curve $15) Here's a reversible puppet that changes from a black-and-white spotted bunny to a green turtle with a checkered back and a squeaker in its head. Fun for early tracking, talking, and peek-a-boo games. PLATINUM AWARD '98. (800) 704-8697.

PEEK-A-BOO GAME

This all-time favorite has many variations. For beginners start by covering your eyes with your hands and saying, "Where's (baby's name) Now uncover your eyes and say, "Peek-a-boo! I see ——"" A note of caution: some babies may find this a bit scary. If that happens, try the game again in a few weeks. This is a great game that helps baby understand that you go away and you come back! In time baby will initiate this game as a Smart Baby Trick.

■ Wimmer-Ferguson My First Photo Album

(Manhattan Toy $12) Share this fabric book with your early "reader." Book contains bold graphics in black and white and color and has two vinyl pages for adding your own photos. Nice for lap time sharing, turning, focusing, talking, and touching. (800) 747-2454.

■ **Visual Cards**

(Sassy $6.99) New babies will enjoy gazing at these two cards with high contrast images and licks of primary colors on all four sides. Flip them for a change of visual interest from time to time as they stand on the changing table or in the crib, or enjoy as a book for lap time. One side has a mirror, another a smiling face, a spiral pattern, and a puppy's face. Birth & up. (800) 323-6336.

◇◇

SMART BABY TRICK

Babies usually turn themselves from tummy to back quite by accident. Then they howl, as if to say, "How did that happen?" Help baby discover how with this game: With baby on his tummy, hold an object in his line of vision and slowly move it upward and to his side. As he follows the object with his eyes bring it slowly behind his head as you gently help him turn. Reward his mighty effort by letting him hold the object in his hand. (Play this game in reverse for turning from back to tummy.)

◇◇

Rattles

Many rattles are too noisy, hard, and heavy for newborns. While most will be used by adults to get baby's attention, the best choices for newborns are rattles with a soft sound that won't startle and a soft finish that won't hurt. During the first months, an infant's arm and hand movements are not yet refined. Here are some of the best rattles for early playtimes:

■ **Baby Bed Bug**

(North American Bear $13) You'll never find a sweeter bee! Covered in eye-catching, high-contrast yellow and black striped knit jersey, this bee has stitched features, floppy wings, a velvety head, and easy-to-grab feet. Soft to the touch, with a chime that jingles inside its machine-washable body. Also charming, a smaller **Butterfly** rattle. (800) 682-3427.

■ Bright Expressions

(Fisher-Price $6.99) Little testers loved this new line of bright rattles with interesting sounds and actions. **Click Clack Birdie** and **Froggie** have soft bodies with bold patterns, big eyes and smiling faces to catch baby's attention. Their long legs are easy to grasp and have clicking disks with good sounds. **Wiggle Bug** has multiple textures, patterns and pull down feet that vibrate as they work their way up. (800) 432-5437.

■ Elephant Sensory Teether

(Manhattan Toy $9) Teethers will eventually find and appreciate the soft, chewy teether on an adorable little red velour elephant with purple ears and rattle inside. But for now it's soft and safe for batting at and tracking. Also charming, a bright yellow and blue **Bear Sensory Teether.** Infants & up. (800) 747-2454.

■ Wimmer-Ferguson Pattern Pals

(Manhattan Toy $14.95 set of 3) These soft toys are just right for early lap games. There's a fish, a boat, and a caterpillar that are easy to grasp. Each has a black-and-white design on one side and a different primary color on the other. All have a unique sound and texture. A best bet for newborns. Platinum Award '94. (800) 747-2454.

SMART BABY TRICK

If a young baby drops a toy he is holding, he will not look to see where it goes. Developmentally, at this stage, out of sight is out of mind. If he has a toy in one hand and you show him another, he will drop the first and reach for the next toy offered.

■ Rainbow Bear

(Gund $10) A cheerful velour bear with a rattle inside is done in primary colors and comes with all stitched features. Small babies will enjoy gazing at him and eventually reaching out to touch and taste. Also recommended, **Red** (Gund $10), a jolly-looking red velour puppy with jingle sound and easy-to-grab legs, each with bright licks of color. (732) 248-1500.

■ Peek-a-Box

(Manhattan Toy $12) Colorful flaps open to reveal a mirror or see-through windows to a hollow box filled with bright balls. Makes for fun peek-a-boo discoveries. 3 mos. & up. (800) 747-2454.

■ Tinkle, Crinkle, Rattle, & Squeak BLUE CHIP

(Gund $10) Like the original caterpillar-shaped toy with multiple sounds and bright primary colors, this update is done in black and white with licks of color and checked patterns for eye-grabbing attention. The long slender shape is easy for baby to eventually grab hold of and explore. Also top-rated, **Colorfun Grabbies** ($5). (732) 248-1500.

◈◈◈◈◈◈◈◈◈◈◈◈◈◈◈◈◈◈◈◈◈◈◈◈◈◈◈◈

THREE RHYMES TO SAY & PLAY

Pat-a-Cake

Flat on his back or sitting up, this is a favorite. Take baby's hand in yours and clap as you say:

Pat a cake, Pat a cake, Baker man
Bake me a cake as fast as you can!
Roll it up *(roll baby's arms)* and roll it up
And mark it with a B *(trace a B on baby's tummy)*
And put it in the oven *(Put baby's arms over head)*
For baby and me!

This Little Piggy

At first your baby doesn't even know where her fingers or toes are or how they work. You can help her discover them with this classic game. Hold baby's hand so she can see her fingers and say:

This Little Piggy went to market *(touch her thumb)*
This Little Piggy stayed home *(touch pointer finger)*
This Little Piggy had roast beef *(touch middle finger)*
This Little Piggy had none *(touch ring finger)*
And this Little Piggy went *(touch pinkie finger)*
WEE, WEE, WEE all the way home! *(run your fingers up baby's arm and tickle her under the chin!)*

Play this with the other hand and then the toesies.

Going To Kentucky

You can gently exercise baby's arms and legs as you say and play this entertaining song:
(move baby's legs in a bike riding action as you sing)
We're going to Kentucky
We're going to the fair
To see a señorita
with flowers in her hair

(now, take baby's hands & roll them over her chest)
Oh, shake it, shake it, shake it
Shake it up and down
Shake it like a milkshake
Shake yourself around!

BABY MUSIC GAMES

Sing, Sing a Song! Okay, it doesn't matter if you sing off key or you don't know all the words. To your baby, you deserve a Grammy! Singing can soothe a crying baby or refresh and surprise a fussy baby. Go, ahead! Add their name to the songs you sing and you'll really have a fan!

Dance with Me! Before baby can get up and boogie on his two feet, he'll enjoy moving about in your arms. Depending on the mood, try some slow, soothing dancing. Or for livelier moments, go on and rock and roll that baby. It's a great way to release your tension as well as baby's.

The Vertical Infant

Once babies can sit up, they have a new view of and fascination with the world of things. Now they don't just grasp at toys, they can use their hands and mouths to explore and feel objects. At around nine months, babies gain fuller control of their separate fingers and begin to use their index fingers to point and poke at openings. Now they can activate toys with spinners. It's also at this stage they can handle two objects at the same time.

Watch how your baby explores any toy, examining every angle. She looks at it, fingers it, tastes it. Using two hands, she bangs two blocks together, or spends many moments passing a toy from one hand to another. This is serious work, a way of discovering how things work and what she can do to make things happen.

During this exciting time your baby will begin to crawl and even pull herself up on her two little feet. Some may even take their first steps. In a matter of just a few months your baby grows from needing others to lead a game of patty-cake, to putting out her hands and leading others to play patty-cake with her.

Many of the toys from the horizontal stage will still be used. By now, however, the mobile should be removed from the crib, and new, interesting playthings should be added gradually. As new toys are introduced, put some of the older things away. Recycle toys that have lost their novelty by putting them out of sight for a while; then reintroduce them or give them away. A clutter of playthings can become more of a distraction than an attraction.

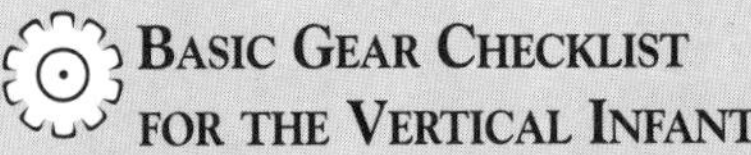

Basic Gear Checklist for the Vertical Infant

- ✓ **Rattles and teething toys**
- ✓ **Manipulatives with differing shapes, sounds, textures**
- ✓ **Washable dolls and animals**
- ✓ **Musical toys**
- ✓ **Soft fabric-covered ball**
- ✓ **Rolling toys or vehicles**
- ✓ **Plastic containers for filling and dumping games**
- ✓ **Cloth blocks**
- ✓ **Bath toys**
- ✓ **Cloth or sturdy cardboard books**

Toys to Avoid

These toys pose choking and/or suffocation hazards:

- ✓ **Antique rattles**
- ✓ **Foam toys**
- ✓ **Toys with elastic**
- ✓ **Toys with buttons, bells, and ribbons**
- ✓ **Old wooden toys that may contain lead paint**
- ✓ **Furry plush dolls that shed**

✓ **Any toys with small parts**

These toys are developmentally inappropriate:

✓ **Shape sorters and ring-and-post toys call for skills that are beyond infants.**

Rattles and Teethers

Now is the time for manipulatives that encourage two-handed exploration as well as provide interesting textures, sounds, and safe, chewable surfaces for teething. You can't teach eye-hand coordination, but you can motivate exploration by providing toys that develop baby's ability to use their hands and fingers in new and more complex ways.

■ Baby Smiley Face Rattle

(Sassy $7.50) A smiling face with jiggly eyes, squeaky nose button, rolling beads, and chewy, polka-dotted, handle-shaped ears reverses for a peek at baby's own smiling face in a distortion-free mirror. Also fun but quirky, **Smiley Space Face Rattles** with green or blue faces and chewy antennae. (800) 323-6336.

■ Ambi Ted Triple Teether

(Learning Curve $5.99 each) The body of this teddy bear teether has three different colors and textures for baby to feel and taste. Also highly recommended from the same line, the **Birdy Tweeter** ($6.99) and **Twin Rattles** ($5.99) BLUE CHIP that looks like two interlocking gears. (800) 704-8697.

■ Earlyears Earl E. Bird

(International Playthings $12) Soft and interesting textures and patterns make this easy-to-grab "bird" a good choice for newborns and beyond. There's something for all the senses on this colorful toy with crinkle and squeak sounds as well as chewable rings for teething. PLATINUM AWARD '99. Birth & up. Also highly recommended for teething from the same line, **Chewing Rings** ($9.95). (800) 445-8347.

■ Early Start Red Rings Blue Chip

(International Playthings $10.50) You may have played with this classic spinning teether with easy-to-grasp red rings that revolve around a blue ball. An interesting toy for two-handed play. Also recommended from the same collection, **Balls in a Bowl** ($20), a see-through ball with smaller flutter balls to fill and spill. (800) 445-8347.

■ Lamaze Rattlebug

(Learning Curve $8) This colorful, eye-catching two-handled bug has chewy wings that are easy to grasp and soothing for teethers. (800) 704-8697.

■ Tolo Activity Cube & Gripper Rattle

(Small World $ 10 each) We were really impressed with this new but classic looking line of baby toys. All are crafted in smooth, sturdy primary-colored plastics. An **Activity Cube** for little fingers to activate has a mirror, beads, squeaker, roller and spinning ball. The **Gripper Ball** has four easy-to-grab rounded handles and a see-through hourglass in the middle with beads that roll from side to side. Also highly recommended from the same maker, easy to grab and chew, **Triangle Rings** ($5), **Abacus Rings** ($5) for shaking and tasting, and the **Roller Rattle Ball** ($5) with plenty of finger holds and a jolly sound as the rattle is shaken or rolled. (800) 421-4153.

■ Sesame Street See & Sounds Rattle

(Fisher-Price $5.99) Older babies will enjoy making the little beads cascade through the see-through portion of the circular rattle when it is turned up and down. Elmo and Big Bird are also inside playing peek-a-boo as the beads move through the toy. (800) 432-5437.

■ Winkel

(Manhattan Toy $12) Finding rattles small enough for baby to grasp is not easy. This colorful "ball" is formed of chewy loops. It has a quiet rattle sound and doubles as a teether. 6 mos. & up. (800) 747-2454.

MORE PEEK-A-BOO GAMES

Peek-A-Boo Scarf Game Put a scarf on your face and ask "Where's (baby's name)?" Drop the scarf and say "I see—-" Before long, baby will pull the scarf away! Variation: Put the scarf on baby's face and you or baby pull it away saying, "Peek-a-boo!"

Do You Hear What I Hear? Put a musical toy under a pillow or scarf on the floor. Turn it on. Ask baby, "Do you hear what I hear? Where is it? " Get down on the floor and help baby discover where that music is coming from. It's a musical version of peek-a-boo. Older sibs like hiding the toy.

Who's That? Your baby in arms will be amazed to catch sight of herself and you in a mirror. Watch her surprise as she sees you twice–the real you and your reflection. Talk about what she sees and let her touch your face and your reflection. In time you can play little games of "Where is my nose? Where is baby's nose?" Move baby in and out of the sight line of the mirror playing yet another variation of Peek-a-Boo!

Where's the Ball? Cover most of the ball with cloth and ask, "Where's the ball?" If your baby doesn't uncover the ball, lift the cover and hide it again. Eventually you can cover the object completely. And baby will look for it. This game helps baby learn that even if an object can't be seen, it still exists.

SIT-UP BABY GAME

Upsa-Daisy. At around 6 months, your baby will still need a hand as he learns to go from lying down to sitting up. Say, "Upsa-daisy" as baby holds your fingers. Play this on soft bed or cushion allowing baby to gently fall back sometimes. Once baby gets the hang of it, try the reverse by gently pushing your sitting-up baby down and saying "Whoops-a-daisy." Learning how to fall over is fun, too!

Floor Toys

First Blocks

■ Enchanted Garden Shapes

(Manhattan Toy $13) Here's a new twist to a classic combo—a colorful ball and block. Baby will enjoy investigating the interesting textures, patterns, and sounds of these fabric toys. The ball with crinkly sounds and varying textures is done in primary colors and has a smiling baby face on one side and a spiral graphic on the other end. The block has a wonderful jingle,interesting textures, and bright patterned graphics. Baby will be shaking, tossing, and chasing these two colorful toys. Still top-rated from this company, **Mind Shapes** ($20 for 3) come in bold black and white graphics with licks of primary colors. (800) 747-2454.

■ Lamaze Clutch Cube

(Learning Curve $11.99) A chime inside this cube makes a quiet sound as baby investigates the patterns on the cube as well as the differing textures on the four grabbers. Interesting for sensory feedback and two-handed play. (800) 704-8697.

■ Earlyears Soft Busy Blocks

(International Playthings $12) We love the feel of these soft fabric blocks that have lots of textures and sounds to explore. One has a gentle rattle safely inside, another crinkles when touched, and the other squeaks. Done in bright bold colors, these are perfect for lots of games to play with your baby. (800) 445-8347.

TWO-WAY BABY GAME

Booom! Before baby starts stacking blocks he'll like knocking them down. Use fabric blocks or a stack of big plastic ones. How high can you make them before your little playmate makes them go BOOOOOOOOM? Baby loves the powerful feeling of making this happen, especially if you laugh it up.

■ Tolo Reflector Rattle

(Small World $6) Colorful marbles look almost liquid as they spin around a mirrored triangular well. An interesting toy that constantly changes as baby manipulates it with a swipe of the hand or more purposeful two-handed action. (800) 421-4153.

Filling and Spilling Games

With their newly acquired skills of grasping and letting go comes the favorite game of filling and dumping multiple objects in and out of containers.

■ Baby's First Blocks and Snap Lock Beads BLUE CHIP

(Fisher-Price $8 & $3.99) Babies will enjoy these toys long before they can do what the boxes promise. **Baby's First Blocks** is technically a shape-sorter, but the 12 blocks will be used to fill, spill, and throw long before baby can fit them into the three-place shape-sorter lid of the container. Put the lid away for now. Long before baby can pull the lemon-sized **Snap-Lock** plastic beads apart or put them together, they'll be used for chomping on, picking up, tossing, and little games of fill and dump. Great for developing fine motor skills and the ability to litter the floor. (800) 432-5437.

■ Dunk & Clunk Circus Rings

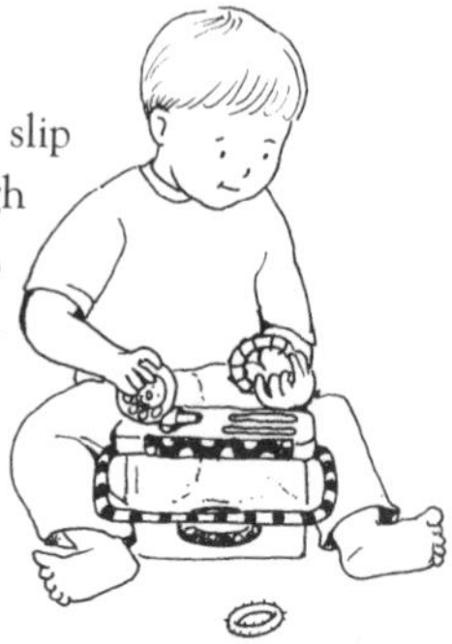

(Sassy $8.50) Multi-textured rings and rattles slip into special slots in the lid of this see-through container. Beginners will like tasting, tossing, and dropping pieces into the plastic box with polka-dotted handle, but older tots will like this unusual shape sorter that develops fine tuning of wrist and finger action. 9 mos. & up. (800) 323-6336.

■ Happy Shapes

(Tomy/International Playthings $13) A perfect fill and dump/ shape sorter that can be used in multiple ways as baby grows. Take the shape lid off for beginners to use as a fill-and-spill container. Older babies will sort and match squares, triangles, and circles. The circles we found take a bit of a push to fit through the hole. Like Little Jack Horner, toddlers will be able to reach into the container's special opening and pull shapes out by feeling them. 8 mos. & up. (800) 445-8347.

■ Lamaze My First Fish Bowl

(Learning Curve $19.99) For some reason fish bowls are big this year! This one rises to the top of our list. Babies can explore the interesting textures and sounds of four creatures: a rattling star fish, a crinkly crab, a jingly fish, and a squeaky crab. All come with a fabric fish bowl with clear vinyl sides for filling and dumping. (800) 704-8697.

TWO-WAY BABY GAME

Give & Take. Once baby can release objects at will from her hands, she will enjoy little give-and-take games. Just don't tease! Ask baby to give you a specific toy. Say thanks and give it back to her. It's a new twist on taking turns that baby can enjoy again and again. Remember, repetition is fun to baby.

■ Lego Primo

(Lego Systems $10 & up) These colorful big chunky plastic blocks are ideal for grasping, filling, spilling, and eventually stacking. Choose a slightly larger container that includes a wheeled base that can be used for stacking and rolling back and forth. (800) 233-8756.

■ Wimmer-Ferguson Puzzle Cube

(Manhattan Toy $16) A fabric cube of black-&-white high contrast graphics reverses to bold primary patterns. A crinkle crescent, squeaker star, and rattle heart with interesting textures and sounds fit into cut-out openings on the cube. Unlike shape sorters for older tots, these soft shapes fit into any opening. 6 mos. & up. PLATINUM AWARD '99. Also interesting, **Stacking Cubes** ($20), a three-piece patterned fabric cube set that includes a rattle block that fits inside a larger block that fits inside another slightly larger block. Baby will not be able to nest the cube & small open block, but these are fun for parent/child games. 6 mos. & up. (800) 747-2454.

BABY FILL & SPILL GAME

What's Inside? Put five or six interesting small toys and baby books in a paper bag or box for baby to explore. This is one way to help baby establish short independent playtimes. Small boxes with toys inside motivate exploration and make happy surprises.

Toys for Making Things Happen

Some of the best infant toys introduce babies to their first lessons in cause and effect. Such toys respond with sounds or motion that give even the youngest players a sense of "can do" power—of making things happen!

■ Bouncing Billy

(Tomy/International Playthings $14) Press down on Billy's head and he makes a "coo-coo" sound and he makes other funny sounds as his barrel-shaped body bounces and boings. His little green arms turn with a clicking sound. Billy's broad-based feet keep him steady for tabletop play. 10 mos. & up. Also cute, his pal **Chuckling Charlie** ($8.50). (800) 445-8347.

■ Earlyears Floor Spinner

(International Playthings $14.95) There are plenty of sights and sounds to explore as baby turns and manipulates this intriguing floor toy. Each of the four cones has a distinctive activity: beads, beeper, mirror, and tracking ball. Ideal for two-handed play and fun for crawling babies to bat at and chase after. PLATINUM AWARD '95. (800) 445-8347.

■ Nesting Action Vehicles

(Fisher-Price $8.99) A versatile set of four chunky vehicles that can be stacked in a tower, roll along the floor, lined up, or nested inside each other for peek-a-boo surprises! Our tester just liked rolling them. Stacking and nesting comes later! (800) 432-5437.

Chime Balls Comparison Shopper

For precrawling babies, chime balls respond to a swipe of the hand without rolling out of baby's reach. Here are three of our favorites—you can't go wrong with any one of these:

Balancing Elephant (Tomy $13) Here's a playful, but noisier, new twist on a chime ball. Give the ball a swipe of the hand and the blue elephant's legs turn and a little tune plays. It's designed to roll around a bit, but if you leave the ball attached to the stand it's a toy that can be enjoyed by precrawlers. Remove the stand later and it has a new play dimension. 6 mos. & up. (800) 445-8347.

Lamaze Rolly Cow (Learning Curve $14.99) A happy-looking cow bobs around with beads swirling around his middle. Satin ears and face make this a good choice for babies to hear, see, and touch. (800) 704-8697. Also charming, **Frog Chime Ball** (Manhattan Toy $15) a soft velour frog with stitched features sits on top of a chime ball. (800) 747-2454.

■ Stackeroo

(Playskool $7.99) Five bright colored arches are designed for stacking, nesting or lining up. There's a little car that tots can run over or under the arches. A versatile toy for floor play. They say 6 months—we'd say more like 10 mos. & up. (800) 752-9755.

■ Stack'n'Build Buddy

(Fisher-Price $8.99) There is no right or wrong way to stack the chunky blocks on top of Buddy's wobbly big feet. Buddy tips from side to side as pieces are added. His big yellow head with googlie eyes can be topped with a bright red cap. Babies will like knocking this over before they get the hang of stacking. A good floor toy for parent and child time. 8 mos. & up. (800) 432-5437.

■ Roll'n'Play

(Lego Primo $4.99) We had trouble leaving this shiny red ball alone. Push the six colorful knobs with faces on this slick red ball and another face pops out on the other side. A good choice for early social games of roly-poly and peek-a-boo surprises. Fun for two-handed solo play and for learning about cause and effect. 3 mos. & up. (800) 233-8756.

■ Pop'n'Spin Top BLUE CHIP

(Playskool $13) An easy-to-activate top with big, colorful hopping-popping balls and a barbershop-like post that twirls inside a see-through dome. Baby just pushes a big red button to activate. Very satisfying toy for a baby who is just discovering the fun of making things happen. (800) 752-9755. Also top-rated, **Tolo Teddy Bear Carousel** (Small World $12) where cheerful teddy bears spin inside when the knob is pushed. (800) 421-4153.

Best Highchair Toys

Good highchair toys buy a few extra minutes before dinner is ready or allow you to eat, too! Our favorite remains **Fascination Station** PLATINUM AWARD '99 (Sassy $7.99) Our little tester had fun batting at this spinning toy that attaches to a tabletop with a stout suction cup that has a wobbly platform. There is plenty to see, hear, and feel as the balls and clackers with bold graphics and textures turn. What a surprise to discover that the spinner detaches to become a hand-held toy to explore! 6 months & up. (800) 323-6336. Also top-rated: **Earlyears Activity Spiral** (International Playthings $14.95) comes with three activity balls that spin, squeak, and go clickity-clack! All of the balls spin up and down on an axle that is topped with a convex mirror for little games of peekaboo. (800) 445-8347.

SMART BABY TRICKS

How Big? Here's a good game for changing table time. While baby is flat on his back say, "How big is the baby?" Take baby's hands in yours and lift his arms up over his head and say,"SOOO Big!" At first you'll do all the action, but before long, when you ask how big is baby? he'll lift his arms and happily do this smart baby trick!

Knock It Off. Baby often pulls up in the crib and side steps about. Learning to let go and stay standing takes practice. Try this little game: Put a soft toy on the crib rail to encourage your baby to side step and knock it off the rail. This game is fun for older sibs who don't mind playing pick-up.

Pull a Toy. Put a toy that's out of baby's reach on a scarf or towel that baby can reach. Can baby figure out how to get the toy by pulling the scarf to him?

Waving Bye-Bye and Throwing Kisses. When someone leaves, baby can't say goodbye. But with a little encouragement, he will delight in waving bye-bye or throwing kisses—except when you want him to do it.

SMART BABY TRICKS

Drop Everything! Your baby keeps dropping spoons, bread, toys, cup, whatever off the high chair table. This is more than a way to give parents exercise. Remember, just a few weeks ago objects were dropped only accidentally. Now, baby can volunterily release things from his hands. It's also a great way to learn more about cause and effect.

Light Up the Sky! Talk about making things happen—lift baby up and let him switch the lights on and off as you enter a room. What magic!

Little Drummer. Pots and pans are fun to bang with a spoon like a drum. Clang the lids together and you have cymbals. Start with one pot with one lid. Put some chunky plastic beads or blocks in the pots for baby to fill and dump. Add another pot of a different size and let baby discover which lid fits on which pot.

First Toys for Crawlers

At around seven months, most babies begin to creep. It takes a few months more before most are up on hands and knees and truly crawling. Rolling toys such as small vehicles and balls can match baby's developing mobility. Toys placed slightly beyond baby's reach can provide the motivation to get moving. But make it fun. Avoid turning this into a teasing time. Your object is to motivate, not frustrate. Games of rolling a ball or car back and forth make for happy social play between baby and older kids as well as adults.

■ **Sesame Street Pop & Go Vehicles**

(Fisher-Price $4.99 each) We love these chunky new pop-and-go vehicles that have popping beads safely enclosed in a see-through top. Give them a push and off they go! Choose either the **Pop & Go Cement Mixer** with Elmo or **Pop & Go Garbage Truck** with, of course, Oscar in the driver's seat! For a larger push toy, we also liked **Elmo's Activity Bus** ($9.99) that squeaks and clicks as it rolls. (800) 432-5437.

■ **Ambi Baby's First Car** BLUE CHIP

(Learning Curve $10.99) A safe and chunky, easy-to-roll car for little hands. (800) 704-8697.

■ **Easy Store Activity Zoo**

(Little Tikes $49.99) Babies love having a space of their very own to crawl in and out of. This colorful activity center comes with a purple door to open and close a gazillion times! There are lots of safely attached toys to spin and move about for independent play. The whole toy folds away for easy storage. Toy looked promising but was not available for testing. Similar to company's **Garden Activity Center** but we prefer this model because all the pieces are permanently attached. (800) 321-0183.

◆◆◆◆◆◆◆◆◆◆◆◆◆◆◆◆◆◆◆◆◆◆◆◆◆◆◆◆◆

SMART PARENT TRICK

Interactive Playthings. In their desire to buy the most up-to-date toys, many parents get caught up with the so-called interactive toys. Babies may enjoy pushing buttons and making things happen, but it's from interactions of the *human kind* that babies learn best. Singing, dancing, talking, and reading books are the basic interactions. During these years no toys can substitute for the best "interactive" playthings in the world—you!

◆◆◆◆◆◆◆◆◆◆◆◆◆◆◆◆◆◆◆◆◆◆◆◆◆◆◆◆◆

■ Lego Primo Caterpillar

(Lego Systems $9.99) Press down on the caterpillar's back and it inches forward with a quiet rattle sound. Bumps on the bright green-and-red caterpillar are just right for attaching a yellow-and-black bee or a spotted lady bug. A jolly floor toy for crawlers. 6 mos. & up. PLATINUM AWARD '98. (800) 233-8756.

■ Peek-a-Boo Activity Tunnel

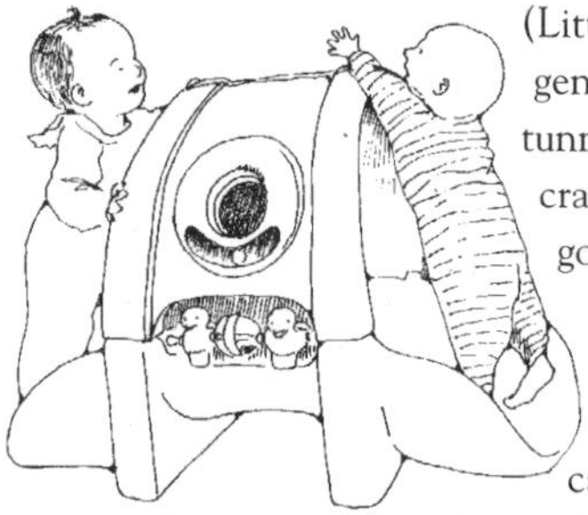

(Little Tikes $45) The gentle up-and-down ramp of this red tunnel with peekaboo window is safe for crawling babies. Our testers enjoyed going round and round again and having a covered hiding place to sit and play with the built-in chunky spinners. It's also fun to roll balls and cars down the ramps. PLATINUM AWARD '96. (800) 321-0183.

■ Colorfun Ball

(Gund $7–$12) A brightly colored ball done in soft velour, that jingles and is easy to grasp, toss, and roll. A perfect toy for crawlers to chase and for early back-and-forth roly-poly social games. (732) 248-1500. Or look for **Jingle Ball** (The First Years $2.99), a colorful softball-sized ball, covered in washable parachute nylon with a quiet jingle inside. (800) 533-6708.

SAFETY TIP: While at first glance foam balls may seem like a safe bet, they are not for infants, as small pieces may be chewed off and ingested. This is also true of Nerf-type balls that have a plastic cover that can be chewed through.

ACTIVE FLOOR GAMES

Roly Poly Ball. Your sitting-up and crawling baby will love the back-and-forth fun of rolling a ball. Choose a soft fabric ball with jingle inside or a big beach ball that's slightly soft.

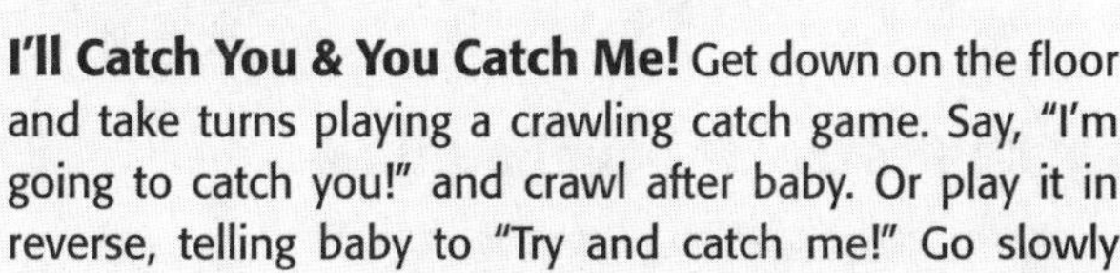

I'll Catch You & You Catch Me! Get down on the floor and take turns playing a crawling catch game. Say, "I'm going to catch you!" and crawl after baby. Or play it in reverse, telling baby to "Try and catch me!" Go slowly enough so baby can catch you. This can be a pretty exciting game!

Tub Time

Bathing a baby can be one of the scariest things new parents have to do. (After all, once you take off all those layers, they're so small, and that doesn't even take into account the wobbly neck situation!) For your own comfort as well as baby's, make sure you have everything ready before you begin. Some babies find a bath before bedtime soothing, others get a second wind. For these babies, a morning bath may be a better choice. Some babies take to water right away, others start crying as soon as that diaper comes off.

The key is to remain calm, comforting, and prepared to get wet! The same baby who was startled and cried when he accidentally splashed himself, will soon be kicking with delight and getting both of you wet. Before long, bathtime will be one of the best parts of the daily routine. For beginners, a small tub will be more comfortable for both bather and bathee. Little ones don't need much in the way of toys, but once they can sit securely, a few simple bath toys add to the fun.

What Babies Love About Bathtime

- **the amazing slippery wetness of water**
- **the power of splashing and making things happen**
- **testing how water runs between the fingers**
- **drips from a washcloth, spills from a cup, squirts from a squeeze bottle**

What They Are Learning

- **using their sense to explore how things feel, taste, sound, and smell**
- **cause and effect of their actions**
- **filling and spilling water is different from spilling and filling blocks or Cheerios**
- **fine motor skills and dexterity as they fill and spill**
- **concepts such as in/out, full/empty, wet/dry are learned in a hands-on way as you talk and play**

First Tub Toys

■ Ambi Family Duck

(Learning Curve $18) Three little primary-colored plastic ducks and their parent (we make no gender assumptions). Great fun for the bath. The babies store in big duck's body. (800) 704-8697.

SAFETY TIP: The Consumer Product Safety Commission reports 11 deaths and 17 injuries associated with baby bath "supporting rings," devices that keep baby seated in the bath tub. Never rely on such devices to keep baby safe. Going to answer the door or phone can result in serious injury, or worse, to babies and toddlers.

■ Lamaze Sea Fun Bath Set

(Learning Curve $16.99) There's a starfish "puppet," a squirting crab, a smiling octopus and a clam shell scoop for bath time fun. All store in mesh bucket between tubs. For sitting up babies. (800) 704-8697.

■ Peaceful Planet Tweeting Bath Birdies

(Fisher-Price $9.99) A floating nest has several birdies that make pleasing tweets when little hands press on them. Mama Bird scoops water and can be loaded on and off. (800) 432-5437.

BABY BATH GAME

Knowing and naming body parts is more fun when you sing them.

Change the words to this song as you bathe baby.

This is the way we wash your toes
Wash your toes, wash your toes
This is the way we wash your toes
Rub-a-dub-dub in the tub!

Substitute toes with hands, elbows, legs, knees, tummy, etc.

SAFETY TIP: Avoid foam bath toys that are often labeled in fine print, "Not for children under three." Babies can choke of bits of foam that break off when babies chew on them.

First Huggables

Babies often receive tons of soft dolls that are too big, too fuzzy, and even unsafe for now. Although they may be decorative and fine for gazing at, fuzzy plush dolls with ribbons, buttons, plastic features that may pull out, or doodads that may be pulled off are better saved for preschool years.

When shopping for huggables, look for:

- **Interesting textures**
- **Easy-to-grasp legs or arms**
- **Sound effects sewn safely inside**
- **Washable fabric such as velour or terry cloth**
- **Stitched-on features; no loose ribbons or bells**
- **Small enough size for infant to hold with ease**

■ Babicorolle

(Corolle $13 & up) A totally washable baby doll with painted face and all-fabric washable body. A rattle will attract baby's attention, and so will the feel and appeal of its velour or knit striped romper. (800) 628-3655.

■ Deecha Dolls

(Manhattan Toy $20) Inspired by young children's drawings of people, these soft velour dolls with totally stitched features are all face and easy-to-grab arms and legs. Will be a hit with the next age group, too. (800) 747-2454.

■ Lamaze Little Knotties

(Learning Curve $5) There are a lot of bean bag dolls around—not all safe for babies. Choose from this collection of colorful bean bag dolls.

These are double bagged for safety, machine washable, and have easy to grab knots and interesting textures. We especially like **Lumps the Camel, Gino the Giraffe** and **Bumbles the Bee.** (800) 704-8697.

■ **My First Dolly**

(Gund $10) Choose either a boy doll in blue striped velour, or a girl in pink. Both are machine washable, with stitched features on fabric faces, and available with African-American skin tone. (732) 248-1500.

■ **My Very Soft Baby**

(Playskool $9.99) An ideal first doll with pliable vinyl face and totally soft, washable pink terry cloth body. Makes pleasant giggly sound when squeezed. African-American version available. (800) 752-9755.

■ **Sleepyhead Bunny**

(North American Bear $12 & $23) These are totally huggable, soft and floppy bunnies in pink or blue striped PJs. Choose either 15" or 8" rattle. The award-winning line of **Velveteenie Circus Animals** ($8–$31), done in vibrant hot colors on soft velour fabric, are still a great choice for this age group and the next. PLATINUM AWARD '94. (800) 682-3427.

■ **Touch 'n Toddle Baby Mickey or Minnie**

(Fisher-Price $18) With a touch of the hand baby can magically activate the cute little horse that carries Mickey or Minnie for a ride. Takes 2 AA batteries. Or for more direct touch, there's a **Musical Touch'n'Crawl Baby Mickey** or **Minnie** ($22) that crawls on hands and knees when touched and plays a tune. While the dolls are not as touch-sensitive as they look on TV, crawlers enjoyed making these novelty dolls move—even if they had to really give them a shove. Three AA batteries required. 6 mos. & up. (800) 524-8697.

LAP TROT GAMES

Once baby can sit up securely he'll like this bouncing game. Put baby on your knee and gently bounce it as you say these rhymes:

Pony Trots

"This is the way the pony trots
Trip, trot, trip, trot
This is the way the pony trots
Trip, trot, trip, trop....STOP! *(Stop the motion, lower your knee, and hold baby as he slides down)*

The Noble Duke of York

Oh the noble Duke of York
He had 10,000 men
(Bounce baby on your lap)
He marched them up to the top of the hill
(Raise your knees as you say this part)
And he marched them down again
(Lower knees as you say this part)
Oh, when you're up you're up *(Raise knees)*
But when you're down you're down *(Lower knees)*
But when you're only half way up you're neither up or down!
(Put knees in normal position)

Variation:
Oh he marched them to the left
(Lean baby to the left)
Oh he marched them to the right
(Lean baby to the right)
Oh, he marched them down to the middle of the town
(Sit baby straight up)
And he marched them upside down!
(Gently turn baby upside down)

Trot, Trot To Boston

(Here's another lap bouncing game in which baby will soon giggle, anticipating a gentle fall.)

Trot Trot to Boston
Trot, trot to Lynne
But watch where you trot
(bounce baby on your lap as you say this)
Or you might fall in!
(open legs and gently drop baby "in")

BABY SONG & DANCE GAMES

Ring Around a Rosy

Somewhere between 8 and 12 months, most babies learn to pull themselves upright. Before baby can stand alone she loves standing up while holding on to your hands. When baby pulls up, sing:

Ring a round a rosy, pocket full of posy,
Ashes, ashes we all fall down!
(hold baby's hands as she sits down)

Pop! Goes the Weasel

Play this for reverse action: start with a sitting-down baby and clap baby's hands as you sing:

All around the cobbler's bench
The monkey chased the weasel.
The monkey thought 'twas all in fun...
Pop! goes the weasel! *(Lift baby up when you sing Pop!)*

Best Travel Toys for Infants

Having a supply of several small toys can help divert and entertain small travelers whether youíre going out for a day or away for a week. Bring along a familiar comfort toy—a musical toy or doll that's like a touch of home. Pack a variety of toys with different sounds and textures and don't show them all at once.You need to dole them out. Select several very different toys, for example:

- **Teether**
- **Hand-held mirror**
- **Highchair toy**
- **Small huggable**
- **Familiar quilt to rest on**
- **Musical toy**
- **Books and pictures to share**

■ Wimmer-Ferguson 3 in 1 Triangle Toy

(Manhattan Toy $20) A versatile toy with 18 high-contrast graphic patterns to hang in the car for gazing at. Thanks to magnets inside, can be hung on the fridge or folded into a long wedge for floor play. There's a small mirror, and touchie feelies, as well as a squeaker that will interest older babies. Still highly recommended, the **Car Seat Gallery,** a BLUE CHIP choice ($12) for back-facing car seats. Hang the 4-way pattern pocket chart on the back seat of the car. PLATINUM AWARD '95. (800) 747-2454.

SAFETY TIP: Links should never be made into a loop, or linked across a crib or playpen. We often see babies dangerously draped and wrapped in long lengths of links. Warning labels say that a chain of links should never be more than 12" long and should be used with adult supervision.

■ Stroller Activity Bar

(Manhattan Toy $20) You can't go wrong with either the **Enchanted Garden** (with sunflower and colorful bugs) or **Merry Meadow** (with barn and farm animals) that attach with

Velcro straps to car seat or stroller. Made of soft colorful fabric, these provide texture, sound, and visual and manipulative interest for the on-the-go baby. (800) 747-2454.

■ Wimmer-Ferguson Discover and Go Playmat

(Manhattan Toy $45) You can fold this playmat into a pouch and hang it on the back of a car seat as a gazing toy for young babies. Open it and use it on the floor as a versatile play environment at home or away. There are peek-a-boo activities, a mirror, squeaker, and teether rattle for all sorts of sensory feedback. Reverses to non-patterned soft side. (800) 747-2454. Also recommended, **Whoozit Playmat** (Manhattan Toy $60) Whoozit's big happy face with a squeaker nose and a peek-a-boo mirror underneath has been attached to a fabric playmat. Whoozit has seven arms with textured rings and squeakers at the end of each for baby to explore. The whole mat folds into the middle of Whoozit's face for take-along ease. Pricey but graphically pleasing. (800) 747-2454.

Travel Toys for Infant Carrier Seats

Toys to gaze at and eventually bat at can be hung on infant carrier seats. These are recommended only with adult supervision and should not be used by older babies who may try to pull up on them.

■ Infant Carrier PlayCenter

(Summer Infant $9.99) This activity bar attaches to any infant carrier seat and becomes one of the most used toys that invites your baby to reach out and touch. We love this one because it is uncomplicated with a smiley little figure that's easy to make spin. Comes in both primary colors or black, white and red. Also recommended, **Sesame Street Baby's Fun Center** (Fisher-Price $9.99) which comes with a safety mirror in the center. Summer (800)268-6237/Fisher-Price (800) 432-5437.

■ **Ambi Swinging Ted**

(Learning Curve $16.99) Ted, the friendly yellow plastic bear in red overalls swings to and fro when baby bats at it. Also top-rated, **Paddington Bear Trapeze Crib/Stroller Toy** (Eden $7) includes a soft fabric Paddington that swings. Both will be enjoyed for early gazing and then as toys to bat at. Learning Curve (800) 704-8697/ Eden (800) 443-4275.

■ **Puppet Play Mates**

(Tiny Love $11.95) How do you get four puppets for the price of one? This innovative glove puppet has four interchangeable heads that Velcro on. There's an elephant with spotted ears, a bunny with stripes, a bear and aboy all with stitched features and quiet rattles inside. A versatile toy for interacting with baby and to use for tracking and talking games. (800) 843-6292.

Toddlers-in-Training Toys

Some of the early walking toys found in the next chapter may be ideal for infants who are seriously working on walking before their first birthday.

Best New Baby/Shower Gifts

Big Ticket ($40–50)	**Deluxe Gymini 3-D Activity Gym** (Tiny Love) or **Sensational Circus Musical Mobile** (Manhattan Toy)
Under $40	**Slumbertime Soother** (Fisher-Price) or **Flatso Farm Musical Pulldown** (North American Bear)
Under $30	**Sunflower Pull Musical** (Manhattan Toy) or **Tolo Gramophone Music Box** (Small World)
Under $25	**Lamaze Peek-a-boo Puppet** (Learning Curve) or **Peter Rabbit Musical Pillow** (Eden)

Under $15	**Earlyyears Earl E. Bird** (International Playthings) or **Car Seat Gallery** (Manhattan Toy) or **Tolo Safety Mirror & Rattle Set** (Small World)
Under $10	**Fascination Station** (Sassy) or **Dunk & Clunk Circus Rings** (Sassy) or **Lego Primo Caterpillar** (Lego)
Under $5	**Snap-Lock Beads** (Fisher-Price) or **Roll'n'Play** (Lego Primo)

Looking Ahead: Best First Birthday Gifts For Every Budget

Big Ticket ($50 or more)	**Push Cart** (Galt) or **Sand Box** (LittleTikes/Step 2)
Under $50	**Doors & Drawers Activity Kitchen** (Little Tikes)
Under $30	**Activity Table** (Fisher-Price) or **Lego Primo** (Lego Systems)
Under $25	**Earlyears Activity Center** (International Playthings) or **Stack'n'Build Choo Choo** (Fisher-Price) or **Earlyears My Friend Earl E. Bird** (International Playthings)
Under $15	**Bigger Family Van** (Step 2) or **Baby Bed Bugs** (North American Bear Co.)
Under $10	**Corn Popper** (Fisher-Price) or **Turtle Tower** (Sassy)
Under $5	Cardboard book (see Books section)

2 • Toddlers
Ones and Twos

What to Expect Developmentally

Ones and Twos. There is a tremendous difference between your one year old whose focus is primarily on mastering and enjoying his new found mobility and your two year old who is now running, jumping, and making giant leaps with language and imagination. Yet, the second and third years are generally known as the toddler years. Many of the toys and games recommended for ones will continue to be used by twos in new and more complex ways. Since some toddlers will be steady on their feet earlier than others or talking and pretending at different times, you'll want to use this chapter in terms of your child's individual development. This chapter is not arranged chronologically. You'll find toys and games for ones and twos under each of the following main headings: Active Physical Play, Strictly Outdoors, Sit-Down Play, Pretend Play, Art & Music, Bath Toys, Basic Furniture, Travel Toys, and Birthday Gifts.

Active Exploration. Anyone who spends time with toddlers knows that they are active, on-the-go learners. They don't visit long because there are so many places and things to explore. Toys that invite active investigation are best for this age group. For toddlers, toys with doors to open, knobs to push, and pieces to fit, fill, and dump provide the raw material for developing fine motor skills, language, and imagination.

Big-Muscle Play. Toddlers also need playthings that match their newfound mobility and their budding sense of independence. Wheeled toys to push, ride on, and even ride in are great favorites. So is equipment they can climb, rock, and slide on. In these two busy years, toddlers grow from wobbly walkers to nimble runners and climbers.

Language and Pretend Power. As language develops, so does the ability to pretend. For beginners, games of make-believe depend more on action than story lines. Choose props that look like the things they see in the real world.

Toys and Development. As an infant your baby was involved mainly with people. Now, your toddler will spend more time investigating things. Some of the toys in this chapter, such as those for beginning walkers, will have short-term use. However, many of the best products are what we call bridge toys, playthings that will be used now and for several years ahead. While no toddler needs all the toys listed here, one- and two-year-olds do need a good mix of toys that fit varying play modes—toys for indoors and out, for quiet, solo sit-down times, and social run-and-shout-out-loud times. A rich variety of playthings (which may include a plain paper shopping bag or some pots and pans) gives kids the learning tools they need to stretch their physical, intellectual, and social development.

Your Role in Play. Playing (and keeping up) with an active toddler requires a sense of humor and realistic expectations. In order to satisfy their growing appetite for independence, select uncomplicated toys that won't frustrate their sense of "can do" power. For example, if your toddler does not want to sit down with you and work on a puzzle now, she may be willing in an hour, or she may be telling you that it's too difficult and should be put away and tried again in a few weeks.

Childproofing: Setting the Stage for Learning

Childproofing (see checklist on pg. 133) involves more than putting things out of reach. It involves setting the stage for learning by providing appropriate objects that children can safely explore. To avoid a constant dialogue of "No! Don't touch!"—remove treasures and objects that may be dangerous to handle. Touching is what toddlers do—it's how they learn. Toddlers who lack the freedom to explore get a negative message about learning. Your goal is to encourage their curiosity about, not set roadblocks to, the world around them.

Many household items are the most interesting objects to explore. Toddlers need opportunities to discover how things work—knobs to pull, boxes to open, fabrics to feel, and containers to stack. A low cabinet in the kitchen with a stack of paper plates to explore will hold a toddler's interest. Pots and pans with lids to fit on and off will keep toddlers occupied while you are working in the kitchen. Toddlers love to take things off of shelves. Why not put on a low shelf their own sturdy cardboard books they can enjoy solo?

Enlarging the Circle: Playmates

Your one year old will play mostly with you and the significant people in his life. But twos are ready to enlarge their social circle. Whether they go to a play group or the park or visit with neighbors, twos begin to enjoy playing near and ultimately with other children.

A Word on Sharing. Lacking experience, toddlers live by the philosophy that what's mine is mine and what's yours is mine, too. It's not selfishness so much as not really understanding what sharing means. Toddler consider their toys almost as extensions of themselves—not for sharing. How can you help?

If you are having visitors over:

- Put away your child's most favorite toys that he doesn't want to share.
- Choose and put toys out that they will play with so

your child is prepared.

- Select things that are easily shared: fingerpaint, play-dough, sand box playthings.
- Be prepared to help with negotiations since kids rarely have enough language to make their own case. An adult may need to give them the language for agreements about taking turns.
- Have a snack prepared for them to share. Tots love eating together.
- Keep visits relatively short. An hour is plenty for twos—always leave them wanting more!

Basic Gear Checklist for Ones

✓Push toys
✓Pull toys
✓Ride-on toy
✓Small vehicles
✓Musical toys
✓Huggables
✓Toy phone
✓Lightweight ball
✓Fill-and-dump toys
✓Manipulatives with moving parts

Basic Gear Checklist for Twos

✓Ride-on/-in toy
✓Pull and push toy
✓Big lightweight ball
✓Shovel and pail
✓Climbing/sliding toy
✓Art supplies
✓Big blocks
✓Table and chair
✓Huggables
✓Props for housekeeping
✓Simple puzzles/shape-sorters

Toys to Avoid

These toys pose choking and/or suffocation hazards:

✓Foam toys
✓Toys with small parts (including small plastic fake foods)
✓Dolls and stuffed animals with fuzzy and/or long hair
✓Toys labeled 3 & up (no matter how smart toddlers are!

The label almost always indicates that there are small parts in or on the toy)

✓**Latex balloons (Note: The Consumer Product Safety Commission reports that latex balloons are the leading cause of suffocation deaths! Since 1973 more than 110 children have died from suffocation involving uninflated balloons or pieces of broken ones. They are not advised for children under age six.)**

These toys are developmentally inappropriate:

✓**Electronic educational drill toys**

✓**Shape-sorters with more than three shapes**

✓**Battery-operated ride-ons**

✓**Most pedal toys**

Active Physical Play

Between 12 and 15 months most babies start toddling. At first, they side step from one piece of furniture to another. Soon, with arms used for balance they take their first independent steps. In these first months of the second year they grow from those thrilling wobbly first steps to sure-footed adventurers. Few toys lend the kind of security you give as you extend your hands to assure him you are there to catch him.

Even when they are able to step along, beginning walkers like the security of holding on for stability. They'll get miles of use from a low-to-the-ground, stable wheeled toy. The products on the market are not created equal. Here are some basic things to look for:

- The wobbly toddler may use the toy to pull up on, so you'll want to find one that is weighted and won't tip easily.
- Try before you buy. Some ride-ons are scaled for tall kids, others for small kids.
- Toddlers do not need battery-powered ride-ons! Encourage foot power, not push-button action!

- Toddlers are not ready for pedals. Few have the coordination to use pedals before 2½. Four wheels and two feet on the ground are best.
- Toys with loud and constant sound effects may be appealing in the store, but can become annoying in tight spaces.

SMART LITTLE TODDLER TRICK

Wobbly walkers start out by using furniture to go "cruising" from one piece to another. Before long they'll cruise back and forth between two adults if you sit relatively close to each other. What an adventure! You are providing the security, just by being there with a hand, if needed. Instead of roly poly ball, it's the wobbly toddly tot trick.

For Younger Toddlers:

■ Grow'n'Go Walker Mower

(Tyco $24.99) Our newly walking tester loved pushing this sturdy plastic mower that makes a poppity noise when pushed. Elmo, on the top of the mower, also bobs up and down as it goes. Well-balanced for new walkers. (800) 488-8697.

■ Push Cart

(Galt $79.95) This recently re-styled classic wooden cart is pricier than any of its plastic counterparts but can be passed down to younger siblings! Very stable for early walkers and a perfect first wagon for carting treasures. (800) 899-4258.

Wagons, Prams, & Ride-ons for Steady-on-their-Feet Toddlers

■ Baby Walker

(Lego Primo $25) Lego's bright plastic pushing wagon is not weighted and is designed for steady walkers—young toddlers for moving about with cargo. 1 & up. (800) 233-8756.

■ Bigger Family Construction Wagon with Blocks

(Step 2 $29.99) Bright yellow wagon with a flat cargo bed is ideal for carting about blocks and other favorite treasures. Four chunky wheels make a clicking sound when pushed or pulled with sturdy blue handle. Comes with two Bigger Family people. They say 1 & up; best suited for steady walkers. **Push About Fire Truck** (Step 2 $20) comes with a pull or push handle for pulling or pushing this big truck that's scaled for early pretend play. PLATINUM AWARD '98. (800) 347-8372.

First Ride-Ons

■ Bigger Family Shuttle Bus Ride-On

(Step 2 $29.99) Our almost-two-year-old tester not only loves riding this straddle-and-drive vehicle, he loves loading the driver and four passenger play figures on and off. The beep-beep steering wheel also adds to the pretend fun. This is taller than most, so test drive before you buy! (800) 347-8372.

■ Soft Rockin' Tigger Rocker

(Little Tikes $39.99) Fabric covered and low to the ground, this huggable, easy-to-straddle rocker will fit young toddlers. Machine washable cover. Looked promising, but was not ready for testing. For toddlers who are steady on their feet. (800) 321-0183.

■ Push & Ride Racer & Semi Truck

(Little Tikes $20) The latest ride-on entries from this company and others do not measure up to earlier versions. Neither the new **Push & Ride Racer** nor the **Push & Ride Semi Truck** have true steering ability and both are harder for new walkers to get on easily—especially if they have short legs. That said, these are now the best choices, but have your child test-drive either for size. 1–3. (800) 321-0183.

■ Fire Engine for Two

(Step 2 $50) Our testers loved the flashing lights and sounds of this bright red Fire Engine that has a rear seat for an extra fire-fighter. Runs on foot power sans pedals and is scaled for large twos and threes. (800) 347-8372. Also top-rated, **Pickup Truck** (Little Tikes $69.99) comes with a drop-down tailgate, hardhat and tool kit for emergency repairs. Satisfying big red horn also a plus. PLATINUM AWARD '98. 2 & up. (800) 321-0183.

■ Cozy Coupe II

(Little Tikes $44.99) The ultimate classic ride-in toy that a generation of kids have grown up with has been updated with a remote key clicker with four different electronic sounds. Also comes with decals for making your own vanity license plate. These add-ons don't detract from the coupe's value as a terrific pretend prop. We have suggested that the company sell the key separately because you know it's going to get lost, just like the real kind! They say, 1½, we say more like 2 and up. (800) 321-0183.

SPECIAL DELIVERY TODDLER GAME

Ask your toddler to deliver a pretend package or ask what she's bringing as she rides by. Fuel their imagination by making a fuss over pretend packages they bring. Modeling pretend games with words and gestures helps tots take the leap into fantasy play.

First Trikes

Most two-year-olds do not have the coordination to pedal a trike. Stick to foot-powered vehicles for younger toddlers. The idea is to give them a vehicle they feel confident on—not one that is at all tippy. However, by two and a half some kids may be ready. Again, our best advice is to test ride the bikes in the store with your child, checking the fit before you bring a bike home. Here are our favorites:

■ Red Tricycle

(Radio Flyer $54 & up) You probably had one of these! A classic little red metal trike with rubber tires and a little basket for treasures. Available in 10" or 12". (773) 637-7100.

■ Tough Trike

(Fisher-Price $29.99) This blue and yellow sporty trike with underseat storage is well sized, sturdy, but lightweight. A good value! (800) 432-5437.

■ Kettrike Happy

(Kettler $129.90) Gender-proof primary-colored trike with detachable push bar for adult. High back seat for added security. Adult testers like the innovative control feature in the front wheel—an optional push/pull safety hub that adjusts for fixed drive or automatic coaster freewheeling. (757) 427-2400.

HIDE & SEEK TODDLER GAMES

Oh, Where, Oh, Where Did My Baby Go? Toddlers love playing hide and seek with their whole beings now that they can crawl, toddle, and eventually run out of sight. They may simply turn so they can't see you and laugh when they look at you or they may hide around a corner and giggle when they pop out to answer your call ...."Where did my baby go?"

Where in the World Is_____? Toddlers see the humor of your searching for something that's in plain sight that they can see. For example, try pretending to search for a glass- asking is it in your pocket? Under the pillow? In my pocketbook? Tots love being so smart they can show you. Funnier yet, pretend to look for him while he is in plain sight.

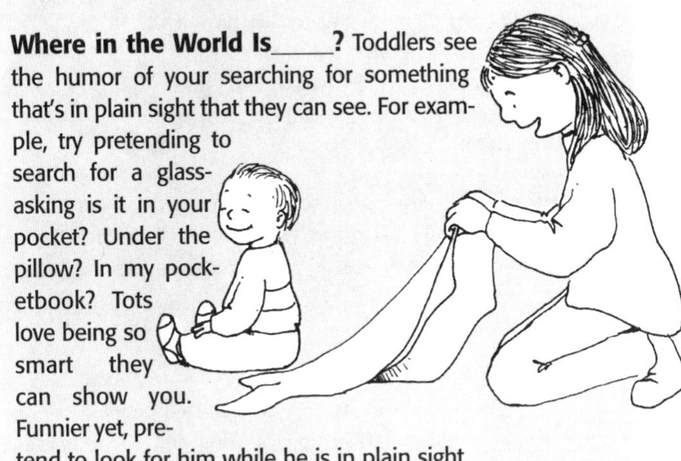

◆◆◆◆◆◆◆◆◆◆◆◆◆◆◆◆◆◆◆◆◆◆◆◆◆◆◆◆◆◆◆◆

Push and Pull Toys

Push comes before pull. Instead of holding on to someone's hand, young toddlers often find sheer joy in the independence of walking while holding on to a push toy. You may even have had Fisher-Price's BLUE CHIP **Corn Popper** ($8) or **Melody Push Chime** ($8) which are still great choices. (800) 432-5437. Some of the best of these toys will also be used for pretend play. Pull toys are for older tots who are surefooted and can look over a shoulder without tripping.

■ **Walk 'n Waddle Duck**

(Fisher-Price $7.99) One of our favorite new classics! Mama Duck quacks quietly and her orange feet flip flop along as tots push her with her little waddling duckling right behind her. (800) 432-5437.

■ **Kid Classics Miss Spider**

(Learning Curve $24.99) This bright yellow wooden spider would not frighten Miss Muffet or any toddler. Borrowed from the Miss Spider series of books for older kids, she spins her many legs as she's pulled along. Fun! Also top-rated: friendly, colorful, and ratchety **Finnegan the Dragon** ($19.99). 18 mos. & up. PLATINUM AWARD '98. (800) 704-8697.

SAFETY TIP: Avoid pull toys with springs and beads that many toddlers will mouth. Old pull toys from the attic may have dangerous levels of lead paint.

■ **Spinning Bus**

(Battat $15) Eight little animal and people passengers plus a driver spin as this pull toy rolls along. There's a ramp for taking passengers off and on. Fun for games of loading, unloading, and rearranging the multiple pieces as well as refining dexterity to fit them on their posts. 8 mos. & up. (800) 247-6144.

Also recommended:

Kouvalias' BLUE CHIP jaunty green wooden **Little Cricket Pull Toy** ($40). This line of toys is pricey but can be passed along. 2 & up. (800) 445-8347. For a less pricey plastic pull toy, **Ambi Max** (Learning Curve $19.99), is an adorable black-and-white pooch. 1½ & up. (800) 704-8697 or Fisher-Price's classic **Little Snoopy** ($8) that wags his tail as he walks. (800) 432-KIDS.

Balls

Big, lightweight balls for tossing, kicking, chasing, or social back-and-forth, roly-poly games are favorite pieces of basic gear. Twos are ready to play bounce and catch. Be sure the ball is lightweight so it won't hurt. Soft fabric balls or slightly deflated beach balls are the best choice for now. Avoid foam and balloon-filled balls that are a choking hazard if nibbled.

SLAM DUNK & JUMP GAMES

Twos love to jump, but when they jump on beds or chairs they can't predict outcomes. Set up safe nests of pillows to jump into.

Indoor Ball & Basket Game. Older toddlers can't always get outside and use up some of that energy. Take turns tossing a soft fabric ball into a basket or small garbage pail.

One, Two, Three, Four. Tots love to count—any excuse will do. Count as you climb the stairs together, toss a ball, as you drop blocks into a container, or take out silverware to set the table. Make numbers and counting an everyday part of life.

Strictly Outdoors:
Climbers, Wading Pools, Sandboxes, Props for the Sandbox, Gardening Tools, Top-Rated Lawn Mower, and Snow Fun

First Climbers, Slider, & Teeter Totters

Climbers are great for big-muscle play for toddlers who are steady on their feet. We saw a number of low-to-the-ground climbers with open platforms and some that did not have secure enough sides once tots reached the top. Many looked like an accident waiting to happen. If you are shopping for a young or especially small toddler, stick to the lowest climbers. This is not a product to grow into.

■ Junior Activity Gym BLUE CHIP

(Little Tikes $70) This pint-sized version of Little Tikes' classic Activity Gym is low to the ground, and will be used as a climber, roof-free play house, and slide. It has no steps, so toddlers must pull themselves up in order to use the slide. 1½ & up. **Hide & Slide Climber** ($ 79.99) This is a taller climber with secure sides, two big steps up, and a longer wavy slide. Designed for big 2s & up. (800) 321-0183.

■ 8-in-1 Adjustable Playground

(Little Tikes $270) A combo playhouse, tunnel, climber, and double slide that the whole gang can play on together. Done in hot colors, this big piece of equipment provides for physical and dramatic play. Parent testers hated the picture of a smiling man on the instructions, but admitted that their 2- & 4-year-olds really enjoyed the playground. Hard to assemble. 2 & up. (800) 321-0183.

■ Kangaroo Climber

(Step 2 $85) This combo climber, slide, tunnel is scaled for young toddlers. There are lots of ways in and out of this colorful climber with Dutch door opening and archway atop the slide. The steps on the outside wall need supervision. 1½–4. (800) 347-8372.

■ **Elephant Slide**

(Step 2 $45) Toddlers loved the look of this big blue elephant 30" slide with three easy steps up and a gentle slide down the pachyderm's trunk. Toddlers can also crawl through the "tunnel" under the slide for hide and seek play. 1½ & up. (800) 347-8372.

◆◆◆◆◆◆◆◆◆◆◆◆◆◆◆◆◆◆◆◆◆◆◆◆◆◆◆◆

SMART PARENT TRICK

Give 'em a Hand! Toddlers love an appreciative audience—don't we all? When they finish a puzzle, dance a jig, or go down a slide, clap your hands together—give them a hand! Keep in mind that little children see themselves as you see them. During this often negative time, try to accentuate the positive.

Bubbles

Blowing bubbles has come a long way from the small plastic containers of pink liquid with a small, ticky wand. For mixed-age agroups: The 12-piece **Bubble Party** (Battat $17) includes wands, trumpets, giant rings, and a waffle wand (enough pieces for nine kids!). (800) 247-6144. The **No-Spill Big Bubble Bucket** (Little Kids $13.99) has three extra-large wands that can't get lost in the bottle! Our testers also gave top ratings to **Little Kids Mini Bubble Tumblers** ($4.99) and **Bubble Phibians** ($4.99) which let kids blow a stream of bubbles. Both make fun party favors. (800) 545-5437.

POP! GO THE BUBBLES GAME

Toddlers may not be able to blow their own bubbles with success but they will love to chase the ones you make. Even if they can't blow their own bubbles, many twos may be able to get results waving a bubble wand with small holes.

SMART PARENT TRICK

For super-large bubbles, mix 1 cup of Dawn liquid detergent with 3 tablespoons of Karo syrup in 2½ quarts of cold water. Stir gently. Leftovers (if you have any) need to be refrigerated. Ideal for large groups.

Playhouses

A playhouse is the ultimate toy for pretend that will be used for years of solo as well as social play. Kids as young as two love the magic of entering their own domain—being the owner of a space that's scaled to size. Toddlers love opening and closing the door, looking out the windows or playing with the toy kitchen (in some models). You'll find houses to fit a variety of tastes and budgets. Little Tikes' **Playhouse,** just 46"H ($130), will be outgrown before their 52"H pastel **Country Cottage** ($180). For grander, larger, and thematic housing, consider the 59"H **Log Cabin** ($250) or a huge

Victorian Mansion ($400) that's 5'H and opens on one side. Step 2's **Sunshine Playhouse** ($110) is just 48"H and has working door, shutters, and a pass-though window. Or for the long haul consider their **Welcome Home Playhouse** ($400) that's 66"H, has a skylight, and is designed for kids as old as 10. If you prefer a wooden structure and price is no object, you'll do best at a roadside fence dealer who also sells prefab sheds. Little Tikes (800) 321-0183 / Step 2 (800) 347-8372.

SMELL THE ROSES GAME

Walking with a toddler can take time but it's also an opportunity to rediscover the wonder of small things through their eyes. What happens when you drop a pebble in a puddle? Where is that daddy-long-legs creeping? What is that truck with a shovel digging? Try to slow the pace with time for just watching. There's so much to see.

Wading Pools

Our testers preferred inexpensive hard-vinyl wading pools to those that had to be blown up or filled with water to hold a shape (most of these had sides that were too high for younger toddlers to climb over by themselves). Prefab wading pools are also easier to lift, dump, and clean. You'll find an adequate no-frills pool for under $20.

Sandboxes

While small boxes are good choices when space is a concern, keep in mind that a bigger box will give more than one child enough room to maneuver. We looked for smooth edges and strong sides that will support a child's weight. The motif is really a personal preference. You can't go wrong with any of the following—all come with covers. Unless you can't spare the space, this is a case where more is more. Small boxes will be outgrown quickly.

Our favorites: On the small side, **Frog Sandbox** (Step 2 $30) or **Green Turtle** (Little Tikes $30). 1 & up. Bigger choices: **Crabbie Sandbox** (Step 2 $45) or **Dinosaur Sandbox** (Little Tikes $50). Bigger still: **Tuggy Sandbox & Splasher** (Step 2 $90) There's plenty of room for several kids to play together and built-in pretend power with a captain's wheel for steering the jolly boat anywhere! Can be used as pool instead. 2 & up. Step 2 (800) 347-8372 / Little Tikes (800) 321-0183.

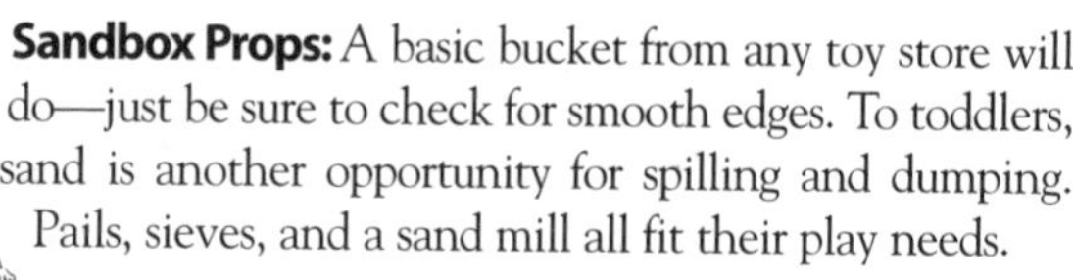

Sandbox Props: A basic bucket from any toy store will do—just be sure to check for smooth edges. To toddlers, sand is another opportunity for spilling and dumping. Pails, sieves, and a sand mill all fit their play needs.

Vehicles for the Sandbox

You can't go wrong with either:

■ Loader & Dump Truck

(Little Tikes $12 each) Like this company's big classic plastic construction vehicles, these are working trucks for the sandbox, but slightly scaled down in size and price. Lightweight enough to take along to the beach or park they have working parts that really lift and spill. A great birthday gift for 2s & up. (800) 321-0183.

■ Little People Dump Truck and Bulldozer

(Fisher-Price $9.99 each) These small-scaled working vehicles dump and dig and have Little People (both male and female) that go bumpity bump as they move along. 18 mos. & up. (800) 432-5437.

FREEBIE: Many of the best props for the sandbox are in your kitchen: a plastic colander, empty margarine containers, strainers, squeeze bottles, etc.

SMART BIG TODDLER TRICK

Shells & Stones. At the beach, older toddlers love to collect shells and stones. You may not want to bring them all home, but it's fun to sort them. Keep the attributes simple. Help put all the white stones in a pile and all the grey ones in another pile. Or sort them by smooth or rough; big or little.

Water Sprinkler

Many sprinklers are too overwhelming for toddlers. We suggest low-to-the-ground ones with gentle action. Here is our favorite for getting their feet wet, so to speak.

■ **Elmo's 1-2-3 Sprinkler**

(Tyco $14.99) Elmo has three different settings, the first being just a gentle spray. (800) 488-8697.

FREEBIE: Painting with water is a neat outdoors activity for older toddlers. A paintbrush and bucket of water produce satisfying though temporary effects—early lessons in evaporation or magic: take your pick!

The Youngest Gardener

■ **Garden Tools**

(Little Tikes $13) Just as toddlers enjoy imitating adult indoor chores, they like working like mommy or daddy in the garden. A rake for leaves, a shovel for snow, a garden hoe all lend themselves to active pretend fun. We prefer these lightweight plastic tools to the more serious metal ones since toddlers tend to toss and swing tools. (800) 321-0183.

Lawn Mowers

Choose either the classic Little Tikes **Mulching Mower** ($25), Fisher-Price's **Bubble Mower,** or Ertl's **Action Lawn Mower** ($26.99) from the John Deere collection. Pull-back handle makes a whirling sound as it "cuts" (too noisy for inside) and the see-through dome lets you see the grass inside. Little Tikes (800) 321-0183 / Ertl (800) 553-4886 / Fisher-Price (800) 432-5437.

SAFETY TIP: Kids should be nowhere near real mowers in action. Flying pebbles travel at 200 mph and can cause deadly accidents. Ditto on riding with adults on power mowers!

Snow Fun

■ **Deluxe Toddler Sleigh** BLUE CHIP

(Flexible Flyer $30) Ready for dashing through the snow, this bright-red toddler sled has high, sloping sides, molded side runners, safety seat belt, and strong yellow towrope. A great winter get-about. Toy Supermarkets.

Sit-Down Play

First Puzzles and Manipulatives

Toddlers enjoy toys that invite investigation but don't demand too much dexterity. Toys with lids to lift, buttons to push, and dials to turn give them satisfying feedback along with playful ways to develop fine motor skills and eye/hand coordination. Without turning playtime into mini-lessons, take the time to introduce a new puzzle or toy. Let your child take the lead, giving help where needed but giving time to explore the pieces and experiment with them. Toddlers who have never seen puzzles before may not know what to do with one. Walk your toddler through it a few times.

Don't worry about spoiling the fun. Children do puzzles again and again. Once they understand how to use them, many of the toys in this section will be enjoyed independently and that is very satisfying to the "me do it myself!" toddler.

First Puzzles

For toddlers, stick with the whole-piece puzzles. Those with peg handles or raised surfaces are easier for little hands to manipulate. We continue to find poorly crafted wooden puzzles with rough edges and many splinters. Our best advice is to check the finish before you buy, or stick to cardboard or vinyl. Top-rated sets: **Kid Classics Puzzles** (Learning Curve $5.99–14.99) (800) 704-8697; **My First Puzzles** (Playskool's $5) 2 & up (800) 752-9755; **Picturebook Art** (Mudpuppy $8.95) 2 & up (212) 354-8840; and **Familiar Things** (Lauri $18.95) Twelve 2-piece rubber puzzles of familiar objects (pictured left). 2 & up (800) 451-0520.

■ Barnyard Puzzle Pals

(Jack Rabbit Creations $16) Toddlers will have no trouble lifting the five wooden animals out of the puzzle tray since they are much thicker than most. In fact, the painted animals stand like the classic wooden figures typically used as props for blocks. 18 mos. & up. (404) 876-4225.

■ Magic Sound Animal Blocks

(Small World $10) When you connect the front and back ends of these animal picture blocks, the animals moo, baa, bark, or meow. A playful way to work with putting two parts together to make a whole, and get an auditory payoff. Also recommended, **Magic Sound Vehicle Blocks.** 2½ & up. (800) 421-4153.

Manipulatives

■ Earlyears Activity Center

(International Playthings $19.95) With just a touch, the rolling beads, clacking shapes, and rattling balls all respond to toddler's investigations. Sound, color, and action make this an appealing toy for eye/hand skills and learning about cause and effect. 1 & up. PLATINUM AWARD '96. (800) 445-8347.

■ Activity Table

(Fisher-Price $29.99) The best activity table for toddlers we've seen in years. Can be used by babies on the floor and for standing at by tots. Table top flips from a surface for stacking with Stack'n'Build blocks to an activity center with whirling marbles (safely enclosed), mirror, peek-a-boo flippers, and chute for filling and spilling the blocks. 9 mos. & up. PLATINUM AWARD '98. (800) 432-5437.

■ Tomy Ball Party Connecting Bridge

(International Playthings $29) Hands down one of the best toddler toys on the market. Two towers and multiple bridges (with ridges) become a runway for ten oversized (and safe) plastic balls that go bumpity-bumpity bump down the ramps. Can be configured (by parents) in multiple ways and combined with the company's **Roll Around Tower** ($24.99) PLATINUM AWARD '98. We also recommend the **Ball Party Pick Up Tube** ($9.99) for beginning counting and the challenging **Drop 'n Catch** ($27) with three trays that kids fill with balls and spill with a turn of the handles. 1½ & up. (800) 445-8347.

■ Beads on Wire Toys BLUE CHIP

(Anatex and Educo $15 & up) Both of these companies make wonderful tracking toys with tethered-down colored beads of different shapes and sizes that can be moved up, down, and around curved and twisted wire mazes. These abstract toys develop eye/hand skills, language, counting, and pretending. Those with suction cups are especially entertaining for high chair play. 1½ & up. Anatex (800) 999-9599 / Educo (800) 661-4142.

Comparison Shopper — Hammer Toys

Kid Classics Hammer and Nail Bench (Learning Curve $24.99) looks like a traditional wooden version but with an added twist for safety—as one peg is hit, another one pops up—none come out. (800) 704-8697. **Earlyears Pound'n'Play** (International Playthings $13) plastic version with four colorful balls. (800) 445-8347. Also very special, **Pound A Ball** (Battat $18), a three-level tower as shown here with a see-through window. 1½ & up. (800) 247-6144. We recommend **Punch'n'Drop** (Plan Toys/Small World $15), a handsome wooden box with three colored balls to hammer through a chute. 2 & up. (800) 421-4153.

■ Sesame Street Talking Pop-Up Pals

(Fisher-Price $20) Toddlers push the buttons to make the Sesame Street characters pop up out of their color-coded doors with a greeting. Each door requires a different kind of manipulative action. A classic toy with sound chips. 2 & up. (800) 432-5437. For a silent variation, Tolo's **Dinosaur Eggs Pop-up** open to reveal a dino baby. (800) 421-4153.

■ Spinning Balls Top

(Battat $17) Push the red hat on the bear's head and the colorful balls and spiral graphic spin inside the see-through dome. For extra visual interest there's a shiny reflective tube and clattering sound as the balls spin. Push fast enough and the balls almost disappear! 1 & up. Also top-rated: **Mini Spinning Top** ($15) with marble sized balls. (800) 247-6144.

■ Ambi Teddy Bear Carousel

(Learning Curve $17.99) Push down on the big yellow knob and the yellow and red teddy bears inside the dome will spin quietly. A flat-bottomed top that's easy enough for toddlers to learn to activate with independence. 1½ & up. (800) 704-8697.

MORE PEEK-A-BOO GAMES

What's Inside? Figuring out how to open various kinds of containers involves problem solving skills, patience and dexterity. It's even more fun if there's a mystery surprise inside as the payoff for their efforts. Use assorted boxes, plastic jars, or containers with slide, lift, or snap-off lids. Put a toy, crackers, or Cheerios inside that make noise when they are shaken.

Which Hand? Put a small object in your hand and pass it back and forth from one hand to the other in baby's view. Now ask baby, "Which hand is it in?" Baby needs to keep watching to pick the hand with the toy. Variation: Put your hands behind you back and switch toy. Now ask baby, "Which hand?" This is more of a guessing game than an observing game but babies love this game of chance.

Where Did It Go? Use cups or hollow nesting blocks to cover a toy. Put a small toy under the yellow cup. Now move three cups around and ask, "Where the toy?" In this visual memory game toddlers soon get the idea of picking the cup by color even if they can't name it. Use this kind of game to talk about the color the toy is under. Babies learn color words best through repeated but playful experiences of using color words informally.

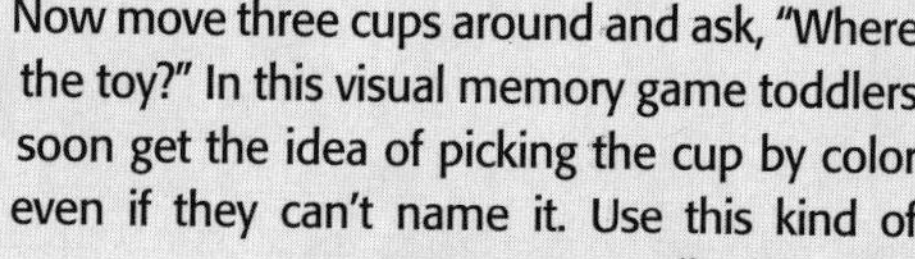

First Construction Toys

Few toys have more long term use and learning value than construction toys. Blocks give children a hands-on understanding of words like longer, taller, the same, more, less, bigger, smaller. These are basic math concepts built into the play. You can help your toddler connect words to these concepts by using language to describe the pieces or what she is doing.

Just as babies crawl before they walk, toddlers begin "building" horizontally rather than vertically. They make long lines and enclosures with blocks rather than tall towers. They may name something after the fact, but twos don't start out with a building in mind. That will come as language and imagination blossom in the preschool years.

Without taking over, you may need to get your child started by modeling ways to make an enclosure or span two blocks with a third. By adding vehicles, small animal and people figures you provide the ingredients for imaginative play.

For the youngest toddlers, filling, dumping, and knocking down blocks comes before lining them up or stacking. Start with **Lego Primo** and Fisher Price's **Stacking Blocks** (see infant chapter). Twos and up will start enjoying big cardboard blocks with adults who are willing to get down on the floor and make long roadways, towers, and bridges. Older twos will enjoy plastic blocks, such as **Duplo** and **Mega Blocks,** and even wooden blocks.

■ Lego Primo

(Lego Systems $4–$25) Day after day, young toddler testers returned to these colorful stacking blocks with soft edges and rounded bumps that make for an easy fit—even by little hands. Designed to stimulate the senses, some have rattle sounds, a mirror, chubby people and animal figures, a wheeled car base, and even a rock-and-spin block that twirls like a top. 6–24 mos. PLATINUM AWARD '96. (800) 233-8756.

■ Duplo BLUE CHIP

(Lego Systems $10 & up) Chunky plastic Duplo building blocks to fill and dump, snap together, and take apart are basic gear for old toddlers and preschoolers. Small sets are good for add-ons, but be sure to start with a large enough set. 1½ & up. If your child is a Winnie the Pooh fan, look at the new Pooh Duplo sets. (800) 233-8756.

HOW HIGH?

Use blocks to see how high a tower you can build together before it goes kaboom! Take turns adding one more piece—and keep a running count as you go. You can play variations of this game with empty frozen juice cans, wooden thread spools, or other collections.

SAFETY TIP: Baby blocks are being marketed in large plastic bags. While they have warnings on them to meet regulations and they do make convenient storage containers, throw them away at once! Large plastic bags are dangerous around babies and toddlers. An open basket is a safer choice.

■ Giant Constructive Blocks BLUE CHIP

(Constructive Playthings $15.95) These sturdy 12" x 6" x 4" cardboard blocks are printed like red bricks and great for stacking into towers, walls, and other big but lightweight creations. Strong enough to stand on, these classic blocks endure years of creative use. Set of 12. #CP-626. (800) 832-0572.

■ Duplo School Bus

(Lego $29.99) A wow-wee kind of gift. Older toddlers can ride on top of this yellow school bus, come to a stop, and use the roof as a base for their Duplo creations. Comes with 70 pieces and room for lots more. A great value. 2 & up. PLATINUM AWARD '98. (800) 233-8756.

■ Duplo Circus Freeways

(Lego $14.99) Advanced Duplo builders can combine constructions with the special elevated "roadway" pieces that little cars can ride over. Putting the curved roadway together calls for some tricky problem solving. Adult help will be needed even by older 2s. This 30-piece set comes with 8 roadway pieces and 1 vehicle. We really prefer the larger 49-piece **Deluxe Harbor Highway** ($29.99) with 2 vehicles, a bridge, and 10 roadway pieces including 2 descending road pieces for more open-ended possibilities. 2–5. (800) 233-8756.

■ Mega Blocks Wagon

(Mega Blocks $30) A tot-sized red wagon loaded with 75 pieces of oversized plastic pegged blocks will be fun for making big, fast constructions. Pegs on side of wagon can be used for building up and over. 2 years & up. (800) 465-6342.

Wooden Blocks

(T.C. Timber, Back to Basics, Constructive Playthings, Grand River, Small World) Older twos will begin to enjoy a beginner set of wooden blocks for stacking or lining up in long roadways. Few toys have as long a play life as blocks which children use in ever more complex ways during the preschool years. Combined with play figures, animals, and vehicles, blocks will be a farm one day, a zoo, or skyscraper the next. As with their art work, they may name something after it is done—for now the fun is in the doing.

■ Block Wagon

(Radio Flyer $30) Older toddlers will love hauling a load of 30 colorful wooden blocks in this sturdy little wooden wagon. There are just enough blocks for beginning builders to load and unload and use for lining up or stacking. A small red wagon loaded with blocks from the same company is labeled for 1–3 but has several smaller blocks that fall into a choke tube and should be removed for children under 3. (800) 621-7613.

Comparison Shopper—Unit Blocks

No two catalogs have the same number of blocks or shapes in any set, so there's a small difference in all the sets listed. The cost of shipping will vary depending upon where you live, and the weight and price of the item. Our best suggestion is that you call around and compare. Here's a sampling of what a good basic set will run:

- **Back to Basics** set of 82 blocks in 16 shapes. (#133). $124 (800) 356-5360.
- **T. C. Timber** set with 87 pieces in 23 shapes. (#50-6674). $225 (800) 245-7622.

(Higher price reflects greater number of shapes with architectural accessories.)

- **Constructive Playthings** set of 85 pieces in 15 shapes. (#CP-U-305L). $169 (800) 832-0572.
- **Grand River** Super Set of 101 dark hardwood blocks includes 88 pieces in 16 shapes plus a 7-piece Roman arch and 6 classical columns. (#A60) $88 (800) 567-5600.
- **Small World** set of 50 unit blocks in 9 shapes comes in sturdy cardboard box with rope handles for storage. (*829739) ($50) (800) 421-4153.

Shopping Tip: Wooden Train Sets

It's a great temptation to buy wooden train sets for older twos—but be forewarned, most have small figures and other small parts that make them dangerous for kids under three who still mouth their toys. Test the pieces in a choke tube or use the toilet paper roller test—if a toy slides through, it fails! Learning Curve's trains and accessories (800) 704-8697 tend to be bigger than the classic Brio trains (888) 274-6869. Since they are compatible you can mix and match as your child grows. Keep in mind, two year olds can't put the track together or enjoy these as much as a three/four year old. But, if you just can't wait, be sure to remove any small figures!

FILLING & SPILLING GAMES

Just as toddlers like to take their clothes off long before they start putting them on, they like the game of spilling long before they get into filling. Here are some games that may encourage the filling part.

My Turn, Your Turn. Play a turn-taking game with baby... you drop a block into a container and say "my turn". Now encourage baby to drop one in saying, "Your turn!" Play until all the blocks are in and then encourage baby to spill them out. Yeah! What fun! Start all over again!

Clean Up Sorting Game. Older twos like picking up if you turn it into a game. Use baskets or containers for like objects- for example, keep all their cars in one basket, toy figures or animals in another, blocks in another. At clean-up time it's fun to "hunt for all the red cars" or say, "who can find all the blue blocks?" Such games develop language, classifying, and sorting skills while reinforcing concepts like color or size.

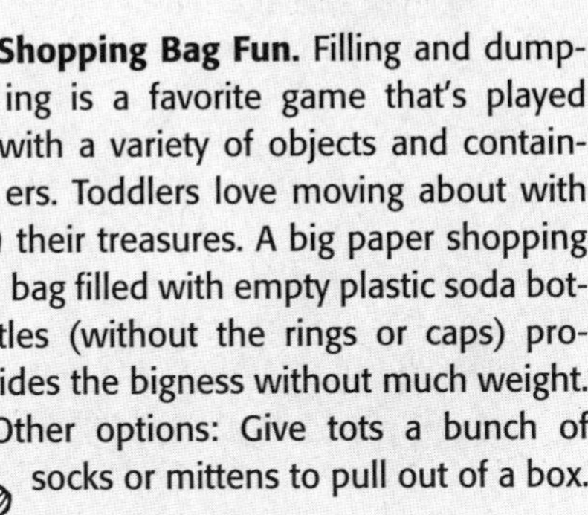

Shopping Bag Fun. Filling and dumping is a favorite game that's played with a variety of objects and containers. Toddlers love moving about with their treasures. A big paper shopping bag filled with empty plastic soda bottles (without the rings or caps) provides the bigness without much weight. Other options: Give tots a bunch of socks or mittens to pull out of a box.

First Stacking, Nesting, and Shape-Sorter Toys

Classic stacking toys require the ability to see and arrange objects in size order—a skill that neither babies nor toddlers have. Although such toys are often labeled 6 months & up, there's nothing wrong with your child—the problem is with the label! We know that some of the pieces are usually lost before tots are able to put them together. Happily, there are more forgiving choices that introduce stacking without the need for size order. These toys are fun for toddlers to taste, toss and explore— just don't expect them to be expert stackers. As you play with your toddler, use color or size words to describe the pieces. Such concepts are learned with greater ease when they are part of everyday experiences.

For beginners start with ring and post toys with interesting textures or patterns like the plastic **Circus Rings** (Sassy $9.99) or the **Lamaze Stacking Rings** (Learning Curve $19.99) with fabric rings that stack in any order. Sassy (800) 323-6336 / Learning Curve (800) 704-8697.

Slightly more advanced players will enjoy either **Mr. Potato Head Wacky Stack** (Playskool $9.99) or **Stack 'n Build Animal Mix-ups** (Fisher-Price $9.99). Both involve stacking body parts – not just shapes. Mr. Potato Head's features are molded into four interchangeable rings. There's a logic to putting eyes, nose and mouth in order- although older tots will see the humor of making upside-down faces. With **Stack'n'Build,** tots can mix or match colors to create wacky critters. Both say 1 & up; we'd say more like 2 & up. Playskool (800) 752-9755 / Fisher-Price (800) 432-5437.

For more challenging stacking, consider **Tolo Stacking Clown** (Small World $10) a four-piece set with cube, barrel, ball, and cone that balance in various ways, or Tomy's **Happy Stack** (International Playthings $13) with a rattle ball face that hides under the five dome-shaped rings, or flip them over and balance the ball on top. Small World

(800) 421-4153 / International Playthings (800) 445-8347. Also top-rated, **Stacking King** (Jack Rabbit Creations $24), a beautifully painted wooden stacker with peg and hole fittings so that all pieces except the crown fit in any order. (800) 445-8347.

Nesting and Stacking Toys

Toddlers like the multiple pieces for pulling apart, banging, and stacking long before they can nest them. In fact they'll knock them down long before they can fit them together. Eventually stacking and nesting toys develop hand/eye coordination, size order concepts, and even counting skills. They provide hands-on experience with concepts like bigger, smaller, taller, inside, under, top, bottom—to name but a few. You can make the language connection as you play together.

Here are some good choices: For beginners, try **Stacking Cups** (Sassy $5.50) Four boldly patterned cups with interesting textures on the rims. 1 & up. (800) 323-6336. **Sort & Stack Set** (Battat $13) a 10-piece set, has large tubs and a handful of shapes that fit through a sorter lid on the largest tub. (800) 247-6144. For a classic set of nesting cups the **Stack 'm Up Cups** (First Years $5.99) have rolled edges and numerals embossed on the bottom of the 10 colorful cups that will be used in tub, sandbox, or for hide-and-seek shell games. 1 & up. (800) 533-6708. **Ambi Nesting Boxes** (Learning Curve $9.99) are six plastic boxes with lids for matching. 2 & up. (800) 704-8697. **Tot Tower** (eeboo $19) Handsome cardboard nesting blocks with familiar objects to know and name. Their newest version, **Baby Things,** has multi-ethnic toddlers' faces and a range of feeling in their expressions. 1 & up. (212) 222-0823.

Ways to Make the Most of Nesters and Stackers

- Spin the rings or roll them for younger tots to catch or fetch.
- Put surprises under one cup or cube and rearrange their order; invite older toddlers to find the hidden object.
- Many sets come with too many pieces for tots to start stacking or nesting. Use just a few with clearly different sizes—two or three that will easily fit in or on top of each other. Gradually add more pieces with closer differences.

Shape-Sorters

■ Ambi Lockablock

(Learning Curve $19.99) Unlike many key and lock toys, this one has an easy action that responds with a turn of the wrist. Tots fill the block through the shape sorter top. There are just three shapes—a ball, cube, and triangle, and the rim of the sorter is color-coded to match the shapes. Without turning the toy into a quiz, use color and shape words to describe the pieces as you play a "find-it" game. 18 mos. & up. (800) 704-8697.

■ Shape-N-Sort

(Plan Toys/Small World $15) Three shapes fit easily in the wooden box with lift-off lid. This is simpler to use than the Lockablock above. 18 mos. & up. Also special, **First Shape Fitter** ($15), a nine-place board as pictured with tall, medium, and short shaped blocks to sort by color, shape, or size. 2 & up. (800) 421-4153.

■ Little Smart Sort 'n Go Car

(VTech $14.99) A jaunty yellow vehicle has musical shape-sorter windows that play as each shape is placed inside the car. They all empty out of the trunk. We applaud the volume control on this toy, which also can be used as a pull toy. 2½ & up. (800) 420-8100.

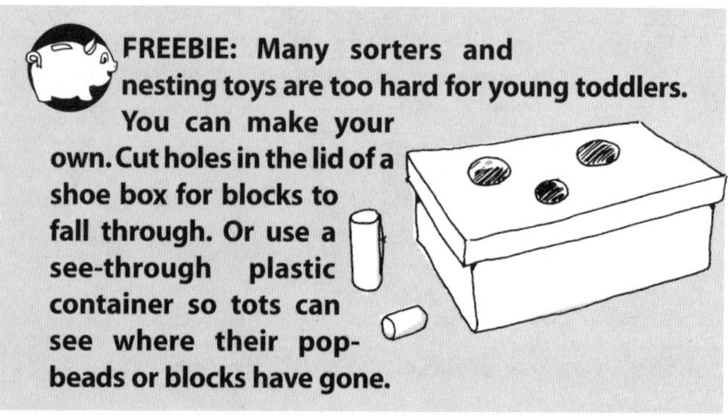

FREEBIE: Many sorters and nesting toys are too hard for young toddlers. You can make your own. Cut holes in the lid of a shoe box for blocks to fall through. Or use a see-through plastic container so tots can see where their pop-beads or blocks have gone.

A Few Words about the word "NO!"

SMART PARENT TRICK

No! No! A Thousand Times No! Why not use your toddler's favorite word "NO!" for some playful games? Everyday routines like getting dressed can be a hassle - but not if you turn it into a game as in: "Give me your foot so I can put on your hat!" "Here are your boots–now put your hand in!" Older toddlers love the upside-down humor of the impossible as they giggle a good-humored "No! No! No!"

SMART TODDLER TRICKS

Testing the Limits Game. "No" comes before yes and is a favorite powerful word that toddlers love to use. Why is he so negative? Think of it in a positive way–he's testing limits. Play can offer happy alternatives to things he cannot do in reality. For example:

- Your 2½ year old cannot give baby a bath–but she can bathe her doll.
- He can't cut up the chicken for his dinner, but he can cut up the play dough that he can pretend is chicken.
- She can't drive the family car but she can go riding in a kiddie car that's powered by her own feet and imagination.
- He can't poke the baby who is taking up so much of his parent's time, but he can use bold strokes of color with his washable markers to express how he feels.

Giving children playful ways to express their feelings provides a healthy release from the frustration of wanting to be the boss of the world!

SMART PARENT TRICK

Do You Want To ___? Use these four words only when you mean them. Too many choices can be confusing to toddlers. Yes, they like having some choices, but there's no point in asking if your toddler is ready for a nap, a bath, to leave the park, or to go to the doctor. Some things you don't ask–you just do. Giving your child a heads up for what's coming next, however, often makes transitions easier. For example, "We're going to have 20 more pushes on the swings, and then it's time to go." Count them out.

Pretend Play

As language develops, older toddlers begin their early games of pretend. So much of the real equipment tots see adults using is off-limits to them. Child-sized versions can (sometimes) offer a satisfying alternative and fuel the imagination of little ones who love to mimic what they see you doing. Never again will sweeping and cleaning be more fun than to a toddler!

Dolls and Huggables

Both boys and girls enjoy playing with dolls and soft animals. For one year olds, velour and short-haired plush animals will now hold some interest. Huggable classics such as **Snuffles** or **Winnie the Pooh** (Gund) and **Spot** (Eden) may become long-loved companions for play and naptime. Older toddlers like oversized but lightweight huggables such as **Groovy Girls & Boys** (Manhattan Toy) to love and lug about. Many children become especially attached to one particular doll or animal that becomes a comfort on trips away from home or for the bedtime journey between night and day. Repeated washing and hugging is likely to produce a threadbare bear or bunny—but no substitutes will do. Bald baby dolls to take in the tub and classics like **Cabbage Patch Kids** (Mattel) with yarn hair and soft bodies are available in boy, girl, and multi-ethnic versions. Toddlers also like smaller take-along dolls that fit in their fists. Since toddlers are still likely to chew on their toys, select uncomplicated huggables without small decorations, long hair, or accessories that can be pulled off.

SAFETY TIP: Do not leave large plush dolls or toys in crib as they can be stepped on and accidentally give tots a boost over the side.

■ Babicorolle

(Corolle $13 & up) When you're looking for a toddler's first baby doll you probably won't find a better choice than these soft huggable babies that feel big but light. Totally washable, **Pierrot** ($20), a clown with knitted face and parachute nylon body, is a bright and happy armful. 1 & up. Older toddlers may especially enjoy Corolle's bath and anatomically correct dolls. They are pricey but beautifully made. 2 & up. Their bald **Mini-Calin** baby dolls ($15) would be perfect for role play if there's a new baby in the family (but remove Teddy Bear!). 3 & up. (800) 628-3655.

■ Earlyears My Friend Earl E. Bird

(International Playthings $20) Our PLATINUM AWARD-winner doll Earl E. Bird has grown into a big toddler-sized pal with crinkling beak, foot rattles, floppy legs with interesting textures, backpack mirror, Velcro wings that hug a little Squeak E. Mouse doll that fits in a pocket. There's a big red ring to hook him into the stroller or car seat. A good travel toy for on-the-go toddlers. 1 & up. (800) 445-8347.

■ Flax or Rye Bear

(Manhattan Toy $15 each) Super soft and washable 16" teddies made of terry cloth are totally right for toddlers to lug and love. Easy to grab with long floppy legs and arms and stitched features, and trimmed with twill bows with a homemade look and feel. Also, **Corduroy** ($10) 8" bear is wonderfully textured. 1 & up. For older tots, **Gigi Giraffe** ($20) is a 20" huggable with stitched features, yarn mane, and long floppy legs and neck. 2 & up. (800) 541-1345.

■ Flatolamb, Flatocow, Flatopig, & Flatoduck

(North American Bear Co. $10 & up) Take your pick of any of these soft velour farmyard critters—a cow, lamb, pig, or duck. Also available as huggables (15") or rattles (9"). Big 25" versions are light but big enough to satisfy a tot's love for big, big, big. (800) 682-3427.

YUM,YUM, TEDDY! PRETEND GAME

Modeling games of pretend can spark toddlers to make up their own games. Stick to familiar actions, for example, pretend to feed Teddy Bear, play patty-cake with Teddy's paws, give Teddy a kiss at bedtime or cover Teddy with a little "blanket."

■ Groovy Girls & Boys

(Manhattan Toy $10 & up) The **Groovy Girls,** soft, adorable velour dolls with stitched features and yarn hair and groovy flower power '60s clothes (1999 PLATINUM AWARD Winners) have been joined by a multi-ethnic collection of boys in jeans and sporting outfits. These are still a perfect fistful for toddlers. Now there are also larger 20" versions that are perfect for older toddlers who love lugging around a large soft huggable. An instant classic—move over, Raggedy Andy! 2 & up. (800) 747-2454.

■ Ragtime Dog & Cat

(North American Bear $24 each) A sunny yellow dog and hot pink cat with embroidered features make cheerful huggable companions. Made of a non-plush felt-like fabric, they wear floral clothes with Velcro closures. Machine washable. 1 & up. (800) 682-3427.

SAFETY TIP: Toddlers should not have pillow-like dolls or toys to sleep with or dolls with chewable doo-dads and features that pose a choking hazard.

SMART PARENT TRICK

As your baby moves to toddlerhood, he may form an attachment to one particular doll or soft animal. This special toy or blanket often takes on a life of its own, especially when it's (horror of horrors) misplaced. Our best tip is to buy a back-up duplicate and keep both well washed and indistinguishable from each other.

■ Wrinkles

(Manhattan Toy $60) Little floor sitters will like flopping over a giant 24" golden-colored, short-haired, wrinkly-faced dog. Also huggable, a smaller 14" **Wrinkles Jr.** ($20) 2 & up. (800) 541-1345.

Doll Accessories

Most toddlers will try to get into doll furniture you buy. Most plastic doll furniture is very tippable. Better to wait until the preschool years for typical baby beds, highchairs, and strollers. Older twos may enjoy a shopping cart they can push about and use for their dolls.

■ Wooden Doll Cradle BLUE CHIP

(Community Playthings $90) This solid maple cradle is designed for schools and built to last. It's 29" and big enough for kids to climb in and play baby or put a family of dolls to sleep. Sure to become a family heirloom. 2 & up. #C140. (800) 777-4244.

■ Shopping Cart

(Little Tikes $25) This bright yellow cart with baby seat is more gender free than most doll carriers. Lends itself to more open-ended pretend games. (800) 321-0183.

FREEBIE: You don't need to go out and buy dress-up clothes. Twos love wearing "real" clothes. What could be better than a pocketbook, briefcase, hat, shoes or scarf that you have really used?

SMART PARENT TRICK

Your toddler has every toy you've bought scattered on the floor throughout the house. Do you: 1) insist that the toys get picked up immediately! 2) relax–toddlers are messy? or 3) use a game for pick-up that involves your toddler? Answer: toddlers can't really play well when every toy they own is out. Make a game of putting toys away.

Vehicles

Although young walkers no longer need to crawl from place to place, playing around with wheeled toys on the floor, in the sandbox, or at the beach will continue to be a favorite way to go. Vehicles with clicky wheels, friction "motors" and passengers to load and unload provide sensory feedback. They are also great props for developing fine motor skills and pretend play. But keep in mind, this is not the time for small Matchbox or Hot Wheels cars, which have small parts and can be a choking hazard. Select simpler vehicles that are easy to manipulate and can withstand being dropped, thrown and even tasted.

■ **Ambi Teddy Copter**

(Learning Curve $14.99) Push the jaunty little copter along and its red wheels ratchet as the round-edged propeller spins and the teddy pilot pops up and down. A pleasing floor toy that combines motion and pretend to perfection. A great companion to Ambi's classic **First Car.** 1 & up. (800) 704-8697.

■ **Bigger Family Van**

(Step 2 $13) Four big play figures—a mom, dad, brother, and sister—are fun to load and unload in the big family van that's scaled for toddlers' roll-about games. Also in the same line, the **Bigger Family School Bus.** 1 & up. PLATINUM AWARD '98. (800) 347-8372.

■ **Elmo and His Pet Puppy**

(Tyco $29.99) Our 2½-year-old tester's face lit up with a smile when he squeezed Elmo's hands and made the little radio-controlled puppy walk and spin. This novelty toy is for older toddlers and preschoolers, too. PLATINUM AWARD '98. Takes 2 AA and 1 9V batteries. 2½. (800) 488-8697.

■ **Little People Adventure Airlines**

(Fisher-Price $14.99) Designed for toddlers, this jumbo plane has a handle to lift it off the ground, two red propellers that spin, wheels that click, and two little people to load and unload. Also includes a chunky vehicle for bringing luggage and fuel to the plane. Simple enough for beginning pretenders. Also clever, the **Little People Push'n'Pull Fire Truck** with lift-up ladder that doubles as a pushing handle. 18 mos. & up. (800) 432-5437.

■ Tolo Baby Driver Steering Wheel

(Small World $10) Attach this suction-cup toy to high chair or any table and tots will give it miles of action. An adjustable yellow steering wheel with red beeping horn makes a ratcheting sound as it's raised or lowered. There's a gear shift that moves, too, and a suction cup that really holds on! 1 & up. (800) 421-4153.

FIVE PLAYFUL WAYS TO SPIN THEIR WHEELS GAMES

Build a Ramp Game. Build a ramp for rolling cars and trucks up and down a hill of pillows. Race two cars and see which one goes down hill fastest. Use the words up and down to reinforce those concepts.

Make a Roadway Game. Make a roadway with a long line of blocks and show your toddler how to run her vehicles over the road. Use simple tunnels with boxes or blocks that cars can go under.

Build a Garage. Use a cardboard box to build a little garage with cut out doors for driving cars in and out.

Take a Drive. Demo how to drive little vehicles under tables, around chair legs, around a corner, behind a pillow. Add a little drama–stopping for gas, red lights, traffic jams. These are concrete ways to develop language concepts while modeling pretend play.

Drive-In. A few wheeled toys on top of a feeding tray can go a long way in making time fly in a restaurant while you're waiting for food to come.

School Buses

We are delighted that both Fisher-Price's **Little People School Bus** ($14.99) and Little Tikes' **School Toddle Tots School Bus** ($12.99) come with rear ramps, wheelchairs, and play people. Passengers can also be loaded in toddler fashion through the open roof. The new Fisher-Price model has googly eyes and passengers that bounce up and down. You can't go wrong with either. 1½–5. Fisher-Price (800) 432-5437 / Little Tikes (800) 321-0183.

■ **Stack'n'Build Choo Choo**

(Fisher-Price $14.99) Fits together easily with the rounded stacking blocks. The 10-piece set has a red engine, two cars, and plenty of other rounded blocks and characters that link the train together. Says 6–36 months. We'd say tots 12–24 months are the right target age. (800) 432-5437.

TODDLER PRETEND GAMES

Giddy-Up, Horsie! Lie on your stomach while your toddler climbs on your back. Tell her to hold on tight as you gently rise to hands and knees and take your tot for a giddy-up ride. Variation on a theme: Piggyback Rides. Riding on your shoulders tots get a bird's eye view from your shoulders.

Who's Flying? Lie on your back and lift your toddler into the air. Few games are more thrilling to toddlers—but avoid this one soon after dinner.

Housekeeping Props

Older toddlers, both boys and girls, adore imitating the real work they see grown-ups doing around the house. Sweeping the floor, vacuuming, cooking, caring for the baby—these are thrilling roles to play. Many of the props for this sort of pretend will be used for several years. They are what we call "bridge toys" that span the years.

■ 2 in 1 Vacuum Set

(Little Tikes $19.99) Some tots hate the loud roar of the real cleaner, but get their courage while pretending with a tot-sized replica. We were surprised to find the classic Fisher-Price vacuum cleaner gone after so many years. This cleaner has colorful balls that "pop" when the upright is pushed. It has a mini-vac that stores in the front pocket for small pick-up chores. 1½ & up. (800) 321-0183.

SHOPPING TIP: One of a toddler's favorite toys is a child-sized broom. You'll find sets with mops, feather dusters, and tons of extras. But it's a basic broom that seems to make the biggest hit. Just check handles for splinters or badly sewn bristles. Never again will cleaning be so much fun! 2 & up.

SAFETY TIP: Buckets! Beware of buckets used in the house for cleaning. Ever-curious toddlers have been known to fall into them and drown. Old buckets from building bricks also pose a problem. Most new play buckets have a new safety bar halfway down to prevent tots from putting their head all the way in.

Phones

Before you buy a play phone with sound, put the receiver to your ear. Many were alarmingly loud. The quietest of the bunch are: **Ambi City Phone** (Learning Curve $9.99) has spinning faces, a mirror, a good clicking sound, and lots of buttons to push. (800) 704-8697; **Pocket Phone** (Chicco $10). (800) 421-4153; and **Tolo Mobile Phone** (Small World $12) which comes with a suction-based stand for when you need to put your phone down! (800) 421-4153.

For more bells and whistles: **Ring 'n Rattle Phone** (Fisher-Price $12.99) Surprise! This phone not only rings, it rattles and shakes when tots hit the big red button. Fun for early role playing. Takes 2 "AA" batteries. This will either delight your tot or send him in the other direction. Try before you buy! See cell phones for fewer surprises. (800) 432-5437. **Cellular Phone** (Tomy $6) with a pop-up antenna and flashing lights. 1 & up. (800) 445-8347.

SAFETY TIP: An old real phone may seem like lots of fun, but the cord and small parts pose a choking hazard to toddlers.

TODDLER TALKING GAMES

All Gone! When a meal is done these words are accompanied with a gesture like the "So Big" game, but here the hands are held out to the sides with palms open to frame an empty bowl–unless, of course, you have a show off, who puts the bowl on his head.

Uppies. Long before they can say the word, toddlers know how to put their hands up to tell you they want to be lifted and carried.

Add On Game. Add to your toddler's single words by using the same word in a fuller sentence. For example, when your tot says "dog," you might say, "Yes, what a big black dog!" Don't drown him with words, but enlarge upon what he says with whole sentences.

It's for You! Game. Older toddlers love talking on the phone. Use the power of pretend to "call" them when lunch is ready or it's time to go out. "Brringggg! Brrringggg! Telephone! It's for you!" Transitions are often easier if you turn them into a game.

FREEBIE: Now Hear This! Save empty rollers from foil, paper towels or toilet paper. These make terrific megaphones to speak into, and "telescopes" to look through. Who knows how many other playful uses your tot will dream up?

Toy Dishes and Pots

Finding a sturdy, gender-free set of dishes isn't easy! Many sets we tested cracked, were too small for little hands, and were very, very pink! Stay away from sets with small parts, sharp cutlery, and of course, save the pottery and china for later.

Dishes and Tea Sets:

Little Helper's Dining Room & Pots and Pans (Step 2 $10) White, red, and yellow 22-piece set comes with dishes, pots, and utensils. (800) 347-8372.

Tea Set (Battat $10) done in primary colors with a teapot that really pours (surprisingly, not true of most!) and 4 simple cups and saucers with a sugar bowl and creamer. (800) 247-6144.

Tea Set (T.C. Timber $29.95) A handsome primary colored set with pot for pouring, cups, plates, sugar/creamer, spoon, and tray. Pricey, but microwave and dishwasher safe. (800) 245-7622

Cooking sets:

My Cooking Playset (Battat $25) with 41 pieces in primary colors will appeal to junior chefs. Remove cutlery for kids who still mouth toys. (800) 247-6144.

Pretend & Play Set (Learning Resources $14.99) 10-piece cooking set in primary colors including a frying pan, a pot, big grip utensils, and our favorite—another tea kettle that actually holds water. 3 & up. (800) 222-3909.

Partyware Plus Value Set (Little Tikes $14.99) An amazing 25-piece set with pots, bowls, rolling pin, cookie cutters, plates, and utensils in bright fiesta colors. Still top-rated: **Kitchen Ware.** (800) 321-0183.

SAFETY TIP: Toddlers do not need fake food! Since they mouth most toys, you'll want to avoid small phony food that's especially tempting to "eat" and may be a choking hazard.

Toy Kitchens & Laundries

Choosing which kitchen center to bring home is really a matter of style preference and space. There are small single units, to elaborate large units that need their own wall, if not room! None of the sinks hold water—which is too bad. There is also a trend back to pink kitchens—we have noted our gender-free choices because we believe strongly that both boys and girls need to know their way around the kitchen.

■ Doors & Drawers Activity Kitchen

(Little Tikes $40) This is a play setting for the youngest chefs. Our toddlers loved playing with this kitchen, which had doors to open, dials to turn, and a telephone for pretend. PLATINUM AWARD '97. (800) 321-0183.

■ Townhouse Kitchen

(Step 2 $50) This combo kitchen with stove, oven, microwave, fridge and phone takes up little space. Also top-rated: **Townhouse Laundry** with washer/dryer, fold-out ironing boards, hanging rack for clothes, and phone. We wish you could get doll's clothes wet here. (800) 347-8372.

■ Victorian Kitchen

(Little Tikes $99) Off white with pink and blue trim, this multi-unit ktichen comes with a microwave, stove, oven, double sink, refrigerator and, of course, a phone. Other top-rated larger-scaled plastic kitchens: Step

2's **Grand Kitchen** ($135) in yellow with licks of pink is the largest kitchen yet with doors that open and has a pass through window. For more gender-free choices look at: Step 2's **Homestyle Kitchen** ($60) with a drop down table; Little Tikes' **DoubleUp Kitchen & Laundry Center** ($79.99) includes a small kitchen center, washer, dryer and ironing board; or Little Tikes' **Family Kitchen** ($90) which has a built-in highchair. Little Tikes' ultra modern **SuperGlow Electronic Kitchen** ($69.99), with lots of bells and whistles, was not ready for testing. Step 2 (800) 347-8372 / Little Tikes (800) 321-0183.

SHOPPING TIP: If you're looking for a wooden kitchen, you'll need to shop the catalogs. A combo sink, stove, and cupboard looks like a piece of real furniture and has a lift-out aluminum sink for water play. Back to Basics $175.95 / # 2658/ (800) 356-5360. You'll find individual wooden appliances that look like the ones you'd find in a preschool. The sink lifts out in this one, too. Constructive Playthings $149.95 each # CP-653 / (800) 448-4115.

Miniature Pretend Settings

■ Home Sweet Home

(Fisher-Price $29.99) This fully furnished take-along dollhouse that opens up for lots of pretend play has unfortunately been redesigned with lots of pink trim. In the past, we had applauded the gender-free paint job. Still remains a good choice for older toddlers. 2 & up. (800) 432-5437. Also, **Little People Farm** (Fisher-Price $30) This fold-and-go farm comes with eight animals and has four stalls with swinging gates. Note: While the hay and pumpkin in this set pass the choke-tube test, they are, in our opinion, still too small and should be removed. 1½ & up. (800) 432-5437.

SAFETY TIP: Fisher-Price Little People made before 1991 pose a choking hazard to children under three. The company has since enlarged the product.

■ Little People Fun Sounds Garage

(Fisher-Price $29.99) This classic toy has been updated with electronic sounds of the garage (horns, keys, cash register, telephone, and hammer). Purists will miss the simplicity of the original, which was easier for toddlers to manipulate. While older toddlers had difficulty making the car elevator work, the red ramp and buttons provided a satisfying play experience. We thought there could have been two cars instead of one. 2 & up. (800) 432-5437.

I SPY FARM GAME

Older toddlers will like playing a knowing and naming game with the animals on their farm. Say, "I spy an animal that says 'Mooooo'!" or "I spy an animal that says "cock-a-doodle-doo."

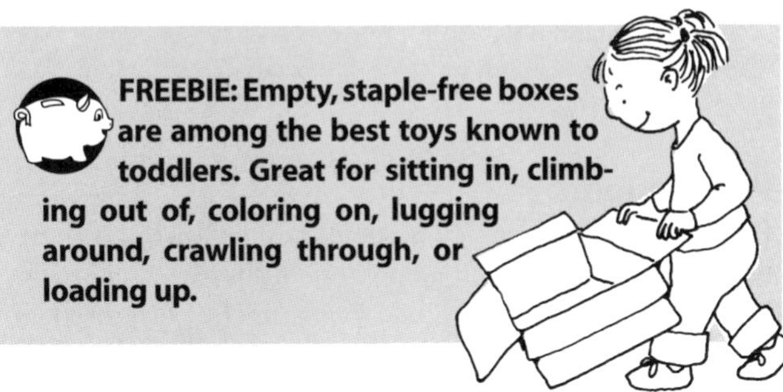

FREEBIE: Empty, staple-free boxes are among the best toys known to toddlers. Great for sitting in, climbing out of, coloring on, lugging around, crawling through, or loading up.

Art and Music

Art Supplies

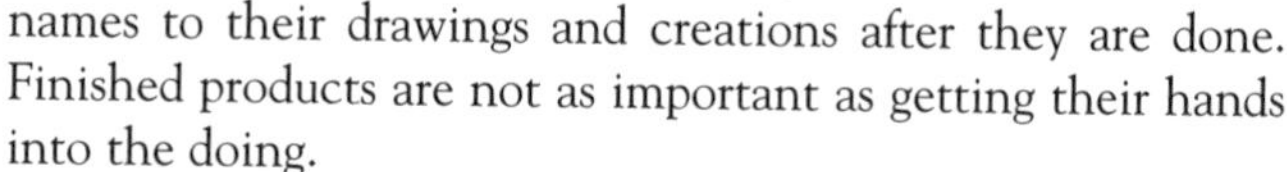

Give your toddler opportunities to explore colors and textures. This is not the time for coloring books and drawing within the lines. Scribbling comes before drawing, just as crawling comes before walking! Twos may give names to their drawings and creations after they are done. Finished products are not as important as getting their hands into the doing.

Even one year olds get a sense of "can do" power scribbling with big, easy-to-grasp crayons on blank paper. Older tots love the fluid lines they get with fat washable markers, but keep in mind, you'll need to replace the covers or markers dry out. Twos also enjoy bright tempera paint with thick brushes, or play-dough and finger paints for lively hands-on fun!

You'll need to supervise and establish a place where art materials can be used. You don't really need an easel for now. A low table that children can stand at is fine. In fact, they have less trouble with paint rolling and dripping when they work on a flat surface. If your toddler persists in eating supplies or spreading them on floors or walls, put them away for a while and try again in a month or two.

■ Kid's First Washable Crayons & Markers

(Crayola $3 & up) These washable crayons are very big to match toddler's way of grasping with a whole fist. Save the smaller crayons which snap in tots' hands for their school days. 1½ & up. (800) 272-9652.

Play Dough

Playing with pre-made or homemade dough is marvelous for twos who love pounding, poking, rolling, crumbling, and hands-on exploring. At this stage the finished product is unimportant. The focus is on smashing a lump flat or pulling it apart into small pieces or mixing blue and yellow to get green. Dough should be used with supervision in an established place for messy play. Beginners will try to taste: It's non-toxic but not for eating.

MAKING DOUGH GAME

Save money by making your own dough with this homemade play-dough recipe. Kids will enjoy getting their hands into the bowl and helping to mix up dough, which can be stored in a covered container. Mix together 1 cup of flour, ⅓ cup salt, a few drops of vegetable oil and enough water to form a dough. Food coloring or a splash of bright tempera paint can be added.

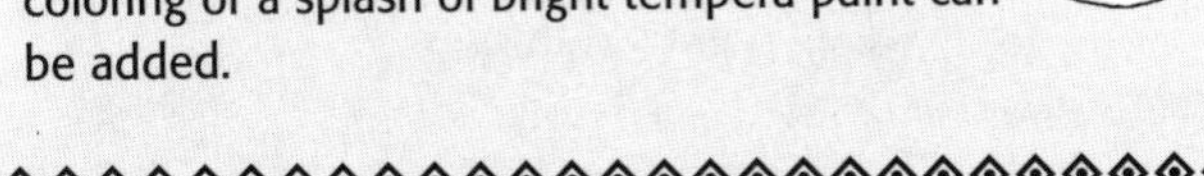

■ **Play-Doh Case of Colors**

(Hasbro $7) Imagine a 10-pack with a two-ounce lump of a ten different colors. Don't let them see all the tubs; open one or two at a time at most. Add plastic dishes for added pretend! 2 & up. (800) 752-9755.

Paints and Easels

Older toddlers will enjoy painting either at a table where the colors won't run or at a standing easel. Start with three colors at most. Thick brushes and washable tempera paint are good choices available at most toy and art supply stores. Try to have the art supplies ready to go for whenever the creative mood strikes.

Wooden Easels

Depending on your space needs, the following are top-rated choices: **Tabletop Easel** (Alex $40) If floor space is tight, consider a sturdy dual-sided table top hardwood easel with four-place paint-cup holder, 16" x 18" eraseboard and painting surface, and a green chalkboard with ledge for erasers on the reverse side. Folds flat for convenient storage. PLATINUM AWARD '98. (800) 666-2539. For a traditional floor model, testers gave high rating to those with chalkboards on one-side and write-and-wipe marker boards on the other (Back to Basics $89.95 & up). We suggest using big clips to hold paper rather than rollers, which our kid testers couldn't resist pulling to create a real paper trail! Item #998. (800) 356-5360.

Plastic Easels

Depending on your space and needs, the following are top-rated choices: **Double Easel** (Little Tikes $50) This bright red easel has a chalkboard on one side and a large clip that holds a pad of 17" x 20" paper. Also top rated, the **9-in-1 Easy Adjust Easel** (Little Tikes $25). Takes little space and adjusts to nine different heights for tots to preteens. (800) 321-0183. If room permits, look at **Creative Art Center** (Step 2 $40). This art center has two easels and a work table in between. 2 & up. (800) 347-8372.

ARTSIE-SMART TODDLER TRICKS

Hot Air Painting. Put a blob of paint on paper. With a plastic straw, demo how you can make colorful patterns by puffing on the paint with the straw. Add a second color and shazam-mmm! You make a new color!

Dip & Dab Game. Cut up a clean sponge into circle, square, triangle or other shapes. Put paint in a shallow dish. Twos will have fun dipping and printing the shapes on a big piece of paper.

Seeing Double Game. Twos will be amazed by dropping a splat of paint in the middle of a paper and folding it in half. Demo how to spread the paint by rubbing the fold. Open it up and WOW! What does it look like?

Musical Toys

Once they are steady on their feet, toddlers love to move to music. Play a variety of music for them to dance to or accompany with their "instruments." Aside from the usual music for kids, try some marches, ballet scores, or music from other cultures. Better yet, put on your dancing feet and shake, rattle, and roll along.

■ Little RhythmMaker Piano

(Little Tikes $14.99) Toddlers can easily activate the eight big colorful keys and make music. This reworked classic has pretty good sound and a carry handle so toddlers can lug it about. Too bad they only printed the color-coded music on the box. But it probably would have been lost before they could play it anyway. You might play a few songs and have a songfest, or just let your tot explore the joys of making their own music. 2 & up. (800) 321-0183.

■ Little RhythmMaker Rhythm Set BLUE CHIP

(Little Tikes $13) Shake, rattle, and feel the beat. These safe, chunky rhythm instruments are perfect for the youngest music makers. Maracas, in bright orange, have see-through dome so tots can see the balls inside. Purple tambourine is easy to play and makes a pleasant enough sound. (800) 321-0183.

■ Music Blocks

(Neurosmith $69.95/$19.95 for additional cartridges) We were very skeptical about such an expensive musical toy for kids—that was, until we played with this one! Imagine five colored plastic blocks, each side wih a geometric shape and representing a different sound or voice. Match the shapes or play them in random order—there's no right or wrong way. Push on the blocks in any combination and you are creating a wonderful musical experience! What sets this toy apart is the quality of the sounds: woodwinds, trumpets, percussion. Comes with "Mozart's

Night Music" cartridge. We also recommend that you bring home the "Rhythms of the World" cartridge right away. One of the most innovative toys we've reviewed! 2 & up. (562) 434-9856.

■ Musical Jack in the Box

(Small World $15) Turn the yellow knob to play "This Old Man" until the Jack in the box pops up with its smile and rosy red nose. May be too surprising for some tots, but most will come to love the predictable and repetitive pop! 1½ & up. (800) 421-4153.

■ Musical Maracas

(Brio $24) Shake and rattle these bright plastic maracas with dial to turn, button to slide, and flute mouthpiece to toot. 2 & up. (888) 274-6869.

FOLLOW THE LEADER TODDLER GAME

Use a full-length mirror to play a "can you do-what-I-do?" game. Use big and little motions from faces to toes. Getting kids to copy what you are doing is more than fun. It helps kids begin to focus on details and translate what they see into actions. Demo a sequence of two motions—pat your head and then your tummy. Can he remember two motions? How about three?

FROM NOSE TO TOES GAME

(Sing to the tune of "A Hunting We Will Go")
Oh, where is (child's name) 's nose?
Oh where is ___'s nose?
Hi ho the cherry oh
I see __'s nose!

(Substitute other body parts as you sing this again.)

■ **Song Magic Banjo**

(Playskool $29.99) An innovative use of motion activation makes this stringless banjo with Barney motif a hit with toddlers. Activated when player waves hand in the center of the banjo. Plays 8 instruments and 8 different tunes including "I Love You." Comes with 3AA batteries. 2–5. PLATINUM AWARD '99. (800) 752-9755.

RHYMES & SONGS TO SING & PLAY

If You're Happy and You Know It *Here's an open-ended song game in which kids can dream up actions and identify the body parts they are going to use.*

If you're happy and you know it, clap your hands
If you're happy and you know it, clap your hands
If you're happy and you know then you really ought to show it
If you're happy and you know it clap your hands
(Have your child dream up some more: stamp your feet, shake your arm, wiggle your nose, wink your eyes)

Row, Row, Row Your Boat
Row, row, row your boat
Gently down the stream
Merrily, merrily, merrily, merrily
Life is but a dream
(Make up playful variations, as in "Drive,drive drive your car or Ride, ride, ride your horse)

Old MacDonald had a Farm
Old MacDonald had a farm, ee-i-ee-i-oh!
And on this farm he had a cow, ee-i-ee-i-oh!
With a moo-moo here, and a moo-moo there,
Here a moo, there a moo, everywhere a moo-moo
(Singing through all the barnyard animals is great fun for older toddlers who are just learning to associate sounds and animal names.)

Eensy Weensy Spider
The eensy weensy spider went up the waterspout
(Use fingers to make spider walk up)
Down came the rain and washed the spider out
(Use fingers to show rain falling down)
Out came the sunshine and dried up all the rain
(Hold hands up in air as if holding the big sun)
And the eensy weensy spider went up the spout again.
(Use fingers to make spider walk up again)

Open Shut Them!
Open *(Show fingers open)*
shut them *(Show fingers closed)*
Open *(Show fingers open)*
Shut them *(Show fingers closed)*
Give a little clap *(Clap hands together)*
Open *(Show fingers open)*
Shut them *(Show fingers closed)*
Open *(Show fingers open)*
Shut them *(Show fingers closed)*
Put them in your lap
(Put hands in lap)
Creep them, crawl them
Creep them crawl them
(Creep fingers up slowly to chin)
Right up to your chin
Creep them crawl them
Creep them crawl them
(Creep fingers up slowly to chin)
But do not let them in!

◆◆◆◆◆◆◆◆◆◆◆◆◆◆◆◆◆◆◆◆◆◆◆◆◆◆◆◆

MORE LAP TROTS

The King Sat on his Throne

(As you say this you bounce the baby on your knees)
The king sat on his throne
and he ate one apple.
But he was still hungry! So...

The king sat on his throne
and he ate five apples.
But he was still hungry! So...
(As you say this, keep bouncing the baby on your knees)

The king sat on his throne
and he at a barrel of apples and he went...
(As you say this, keep bouncing the baby on your knees)
KABOOM!
(Drop baby gently between your knees as you say "Kaboom!")

(Play variations of this game using various kinds of fruits and other food baby likes. It's not knowing when the "Kaboom!" will come that makes this so exciting to toddlers.)

Ride a Cock Horse

(Bounce baby on your knee as you say this rhyme.)

Ride a cock horse to Banbury Cross
To see a great lady upon a great horse.
Rings on her fingers, and bells on her toes,
She shall have music wherever she goes.

Bath Toys

For young bathers, tub time is just another locale for learning and play. Working up a lather, trying to keep a slippery soap from slipping away, discovering how water spills from a cup, drips from a washcloth, and splashes when you hit it—these are a child's way of finding out how things like soap and water work. In or out of the tub, toddlers are becoming great pretenders. Simple toys like small buckets, boats, a rubber ducky, or a tubbable doll all invite the kind of imaginative play older toddlers like best. Tub time is also a good time for chanting nursery rhymes like "Rub-a-dub-dub, three men in a tub." For the sometimes reluctant bather, a new toy or a game will do the trick.

SAFETY TIP: Foam bath toys are a choking hazard to toddlers, who may bite off pieces. Unfortunately, many of the age labels on such products are in very small print.

■ Lamaze Tub Frogs

(Learning Curve $17.99) There's a big green lilypad that floats and holds three frogs, each of which squirts in a different way, and a "bug" with wings that spin when it's pulled through the water. 1½ & up. (800) 704-8697.

■ Scoop 'n Squirt Fun Pack

(Lego $17.99) For tub time or wading pool this set adds dandy fun. There's a squirting frog, a paddling turtle, an easy-to-grasp floating starfish, two waterbugs, two Lego Primo people that float on a Lily Pad, and a ducky boat. Scoop them all out with a big-handled yellow and red mesh net that holds them till the next tub. Looked promising, but was not available for testing. 6 mos. & up. (800) 233-8756.

■ Splash Along Teddy & Swimmers

(Tomy/International Plathings $7) Here are two small but delightful tub toys to tempt a reluctant bather into the tub. Wind the fish under the barrel and the little blue bear on a barrel goes splish-splashing around the tub. Or press the tail fin on the friendly little blue shark **Swimmers**

($5) and it paddles across the tub. 18 mos. & up. (800) 445-8347.

■ Turtle Tower

(Sassy $8) Three friendly turtles stack on a center post base that attaches to the side of the tub with two large suction cups. The turtles which have different size drain holes, are fun for pretend play as well as scooping and pouring water. The best part of the toy is the funnel in the center post that spins as water runs through it! One of the best tub toys we've seen in a long time! 1 & up. PLATINUM AWARD '99. (800) 323-6336.

■ Water Symphony

(Tomy $19) Tap the head of each colorful dolphin and it "sings" its own musical note. Put all eight together and you have a scale! O.K., so it's not great music, but it's fun! Dolphins can float free or in their matching inner tubes that can be linked together in a circle or long line. A clever tub toy for 2s & up. (800) 445-8347.

■ Ambi Fishwheel

(Learning Curve $14.99) Pour water into the top and the water wheel will make the three red-and-yellow fish spin. Combines pouring with small lessons in cause and effect (800) 704-8697.

◆◆◆◆◆◆◆◆◆◆◆◆◆◆◆◆◆◆◆◆◆◆◆◆◆◆◆◆

THE COUNT DOWN—SUDS BE GONE! GAME

Rinsing suds out of hair is sometimes worrisome to kids. Let kids know how long they will have to count before all the soap is out. Try counting one hippopotamus, two rhinoceros... in order to slow down the count, or have your child guess how many cups of water it will take to get the job done. With kids who are fretful about shampooing, you may want to do their hair in the sink, instead of making bath time a hassle.

DOES IT FLOAT? GAME

Gather things like a paper cup, paper dish, plastic blocks, a comb, a bar of soap, a plastic spoon that are safe but interesting. Challenge your child to discover which things float and which sink? Make a float and sink pile for keeping track. Try floating a dry wash cloth on the water. How long does it stay afloat? What makes it sink? Put a sponge on the water. Now add plastic building blocks. How many can you float before the sponge goes down? A good game for older twos.

SMART TODDLER TRICK

Roll It Out Caper. At least one roll of toilet paper is likely to be unspun during this year. It will be very quiet. You may be on the phone or making the bed. It does not take as long as you might think. Your little scientist is doing a motion study and learning a bit more about cause and effect. Variation: The "Pull All the Tissues Out of the Box" Caper. This is not counting exactly–consider it a hands on way to learn beginning math concepts like "lots" or "more and more."

Basic Furniture

Table and Chairs

This is a basic piece of gear that will be used for years of snacks, art projects, and tea parties. Best bets are going to have steady legs and a washable surface. After that, it's a matter of budget and style to fit your home. Check the underside of tables and chairs for smooth finishes that won't snag little fingers. Twos also enjoy a rocking or arm chair scaled to their size.

2 & up.

Some basic safety and design questions you may want to check:

 Can your child get on and off chairs/bench easily?

 Is this a set that will work when your child gets a little bigger?

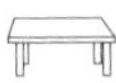 If you're looking at a wooden set, are there exposed screws or nuts (check the underside) that can cut your child?

 Is the surface washable and ready for abuse? (A beautiful painted piece will be destroyed by paint, play-dough, crayons, etc.)

Comparison Shopper—Plastic Folding Tables

We compared Fisher Price and Little Tikes foldable plastic tables. Little Tikes **Easy Store Picnic Table** ($59.99) rectangular table is easier to fold away. However, testers report that Fisher-Price's round **Grow-With-Me Patio Table** ($55) is easier for smaller children to use. The Little Tikes model requires kids to step over the plastic that connects the bench to the table. Fisher-Price has no such barrier, making it easier for toddlers to use independently. Fisher-Price (800) 432-5437 / Little Tikes (800) 321-0183.

SMART PARENT TRICKS

Flying Spoons Trick. Spoons that fly like planes into the mouths of babes are often greeted with sealed lips and firm resolve to get out of the high chair. Getting toddlers to finish their meals can be a challenge—there's so much to see and do and being confined to a high chair gets in the way of their action game plan. Some alternative game plans: Smaller meals with finger food that tots can handle with greater independence can help. Older twos are often happier to eat at their own low-to-the-ground table, too.

Selecting Backyard Gym Sets

Buying a backyard gym is an investment in years of active fun that calls for care before you buy, as well as proper installation, maintenance, and supervision. Having such equipment right outside your own door provides an open-ended invitation to get out and use those muscles and that endless energy. Although the primary attraction may be the swing and slide, often these hold less long-term interest than the playhouse/climber, which is used for exercising both body and imagination.

Here are some tips on choosing equipment, installing it, and supervising its use. Shop where you can see and compare gym sets that are set up. Ask yourself:

- Is the set sturdy?
- If it's wooden, is it smooth or likely to turn splintery? Is it made with pressure-treated wood? If so, you should know that the Consumer Safety Commission now reports that the quantity of chemicals used is not considered hazardous.
- Whether it's wood, metal, or plastic, are there sharp or rough edges?
- Are the swing seats like soft straps that conform to a child's body? These are safer and easier to get on and off.
- If swings are hung on chains, are they sealed in vinyl so they won't pinch fingers?
- Are the spaces between ladder rungs wide enough so a child's head can't get caught? All openings should be at least 9". Avoid sets with climbing bars that run the length of the set above the swings.

- Is the bottom of the slide no more than 12" off the ground?
- Are nuts and bolts embedded so they can't snag fingers and clothing?
- Is the set scaled to your child's physical and developmental needs? Many sets come with climbers and slides that are not really appropriate for preschoolers. Do platforms have guardrails?
- What's the weight capacity recommended by the manufacturer?
- Who will install the set and how will it be anchored? Sets should be installed with stakes or in concrete "footings" so they won't tip, and on surfaces such as sand or wood chips 6"–12" deep to cushion falls. Grass is no longer considered safe enough for falls.
- Do you really have room for it? Equipment should be at least six feet from fences, buildings, or anything that could endanger kids.
- What's your budget? Most of the basic wooden sets start at $500, but that's just for the basic unit. After adding a slide, climber, and/or playhouse you're talking about $1,000 and up.

Here are the names of several major gym set companies:

- **Childlife.** Top-rated. Distinctive wooden green finish is smoother and less likely to splinter than the cedar and pine gyms used in many other sets. $450 and up. (800) 462-4445.
- **Rainbow Play Systems.** Steel parts are vinyl dipped, wood is chemical-free, built of redwood & cedar. Cadillac of gym sets, starts at $1100 & up. (800) 724-6269.
- **Hedstrom.** Metal sets from $149 and up. Available from Sears and many toy supermarkets.
- **Little Tikes.** Their plastic **SkyCenter Playhouse Climber and Swing Extension** ($650) has an attachable metal swing set extension that also needs to be anchored with concrete for stability. 3 & up. (800) 321-0183.

Best Travel Toys For Toddlers

We ask almost the impossible from toddlers when we travel by car. Sitting still for long stretches is physically stressful for this age group. Having a plan before you get in the car may help make the transition a little bit easier. The most obvious tip would be to try to plan your car travel to nap time. Of course, that's not always possible. While some kids find the movement of the car soothing and fall asleep easily, others seem to feel the need to co-drive the car—staying alert the entire way!

It's at this age that kids do that straightening-of-the-back-trick when being put into their car seats. It will help if you:

- Give your child a heads-up about getting ready to go into the car.
- Leave a special toy in the car that they can look forward to playing with only in the car.
- Bring along favorite tapes to listen to in the car.
- Bring snacks and drinks—especially good if you get caught in traffic!
- Be sure to bring along a favorite huggable and/or blanket.
- Bring big washable crayons and pad of paper in a travel sack small enough to fit into a diaper bag or glove compartment.
- An Inflatable ball for out of the car breaks and when-you-get there fun.
- Small cardboard books they can handle themselves when in their car seats.
- For extended stays: a small set of big plastic blocks or the "favorite toy of the week," one you know she'll be happy to play with while you're unpacking!

A PRESENT FOR ME! GAME

One of the best tips we have for toddlers is to wrap small items for them to unwrap. They don't need to be new—little books, a tape, a box of cereal, a small manipulative toy. Don't show your bag of tricks all at once. Dole them out as you go! Toddlers love surprises and the unwrapping process is part of the fun and a real time burner.

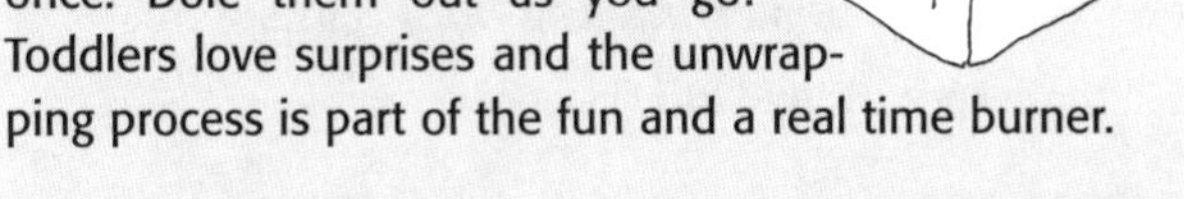

Best Second Birthday Gifts

For Every Budget

Over $100 **Wooden Blocks** (Various Makers) or **Playhouse** (Step 2/Little Tikes) or **Large Climber** (Little Tikes)

Under $100 **Fire Engine for Two** (Step 2) or **Toy Kitchen** (Step 2/Little Tikes)

Under $75 **Music Blocks** (Neurosmith) or **Sandbox** (Little Tikes/Step 2) or **Junior Activity Gym** (Little Tikes)

Under $50 **Cozy Coupe II** (Little Tikes) or **Snuffles** (Gund)

Under $30 **Duplo School Bus** (Lego) or **Bigger Family Shuttle Bus Ride-On** (Step 2) or **Tomy Ball Party Connecting Bridge** (International Playthings)

Under $25 **Shopping Cart** (Little Tikes) or **Bigger Family Construction Wagon** (Step 2)

Under $20	**Tomy Ball Tower** (International Playthings) or **Ambi Fishwheel** (Learning Curve)
Under $15	**Tolo Mobile Phone** (Small World) or **Little People School Bue** or **Airplane** (Fisher-Price) or **Pretend & Play Set** (Learning Resources) or **Groovy Girls and Boys** (Manhattan Toy)
Under $10	**Turtle Tower** (Sassy) or **Crayola Big Bucket** (Crayola) or **Walk'n'Waddle Duck** (Fisher-Price)
Under $5	**Play-Doh** (Hasbro)

A Word about Balloons. Despite the fact that latex balloons are considered unsafe for children under six, people continue to give them to kids in stores, parks and at parties. The problem is that kids can suffocate on pieces of latex if they bite and/or inhale a balloon they break or try to blow up. Yes, they are an old tradition—but a dangerous one. Why take the risk? Stick to Mylar!

II • Books

Long before they can talk, babies and toddlers love looking at and listening to books. The truth is, the littlest ones wouldn't care if you read them the telephone book or an encyclopedia. For babies, books are enjoyed in two ways. For the little lap sitter, books are a great contact sport. They love the sound of your voice, looking at the pictures, and best of all—the pleasure of your company and the comfort of your lap. For more "independent" moments, tots like the mechanical wonder of turning pages and changing the scene. It's like a pleasing game of peek-a-boo that they can play alone. Although they are not toys, well-chosen books are often among a baby's favorite playthings.

Choosing the right books

For your youngest "reader," select books that can survive the search and destroy stage.

- Rip-proof vinyl and cloth books that can be washed are best for the reader who still chews whatever is at hand. Chunky cardboard books that are scaled for little hands are also sturdy for rough page turners.
- For beginners, select books with clear photos or illus-

trations of familiar objects in baby's world.

- Steer clear of novelty books with wheels, textures and other doo-dads that can be pulled off and present a choking hazard. If you can't resist pop-up, pull-tabs, and lift-the-flaps formats, save them for shared time and keep them out of reach.
- As young toddlers' interest in books grows you'll want to add books with small stories about their everyday world.
- Toddlers also enjoy the nonsense and rhythm of nursery rhymes and are fascinated with animals and the sounds they make. Books with repetition and rhythmic rhyme are often favorites. So are sturdy lift-the-flap books with small peek-a-boo surprises.
- Older twos are ready for little adventure stories—classics like The Three Bears or The Little Red Hen. They love their simplicity, predictable patterns, and repetition. They'll soon know their books by heart and correct you if you skip a page or miss a word. Keep in mind that toddlers like to hear the same book again and again and again—so choose with care!

What they like about books

- the one-on-one together time with you
- the sound and cadence of your voice
- the pure magic of the mechanics of turning pages
- the independence and joy of making things happen
- the thrill of knowing and naming familiar things
- experimenting with language and sounds

What they are learning

- books are synonymous with pleasure
- understanding and using language to communicate
- ability to identify a picture, such as a photo of a banana as a symbol of the real thing. This is a big intellectual accomplishment on the road to reading where we can

eventually read the letter symbols of B-a-n-a-n-a to represent a sweet yellow fruit.

- being able to anticipate and predict what comes next in a book they know from repeated reading
- ability to interact and/or enjoy books independently

What you can do

- Put a few sturdy books on a low shelf or basket where baby can enjoy them independently. Steer clear of newspaper and magazines with inks that may be dangerous.
- Select books with rounded edges that can't poke baby in the eye or jab little hands. Steer clear of doo-dads that baby can chew or rip off the pages.
- Make a regular habit of sharing books with your baby. You don't have to wait for bedtime. Books are perfect for transition times, after a nap, or a very active playtime when a change of pace is needed. They are also good take-alongs for waiting times in restaurants, doctors office, or on the road.
- Play little "I spy" games encouraging your baby to find details on the pages of the book. Make up your own little stories that relate objects in book to object in baby's room.
- Read with lots of different voices to make the little story come alive. Don't be afraid to ham it up! Pause to encourage older toddlers to say repeated refrains with you.
- Create some homemade books of the people and pets your baby knows best. Personalized books with extra photos from a little trip or special event are often great favorites. We recommend using the mini vinyl photo albums that photo processing places give out.

Books to Avoid

- Many baby books and alphabets are loaded with name-the-object books that feature objects adults would not be able to name. Before you buy, ask yourself if you can name the objects without being able to read. Are they objects baby is likely to recognize? These are better starting points for learning to know and name the world of things.

- Publishers are now borrowing texts from the preschool bookshelf and transplanting them into "baby/toddler" formats. The format is right but the content is all wrong. Curious George's adventures are beyond your two year old—save them for later! Read the story before you buy. If it seems too complex, long, scary, or just wrong—it probably is.
- We almost punctured a finger on the sharp corners of several lift-the-flap books made of sturdy cardboard. Always feel the corners of baby books since babies can easily poke eyes with sharp edged books as they taste their reading. Many washable vinyl books also have edges that we felt are too sharp for little hands and mouths.
- Toddlers learn from tactile experiences—but they can also choke on them! We've found so-called cloth baby books with buttons that pull off, strings that pulled out, and one in a plastic bag big enough to pull over a head! Books with wheels, furry fabrics, feathers, beads, and other doo-dads often have a caution, "not for children under 3," in very fine print where you will probably never look.
- Take the time to read and look at the pictures and trust your instincts. There are lots of poor choices out there, so let the buyer beware!

Ten Blue Chip Books Every Baby and Young Toddler Should Know

*__Baby Animal Friends,__ by Phoebe Dunn
*__Baby's First Words,__ by Lars Wik
*__I See,__ by Rachel Isadora
*__Spot's Toys,__ by Eric Hill
*__This Is Me,__ by Lenore Blegvad
*__Tom and Pippo series,__ by Helen Oxenbury
*__Pat-A-Cake,__ by Tony Kenyon
*__What Do Babies Do?__ by Debby Slier
*__What Is It?__ by Tana Hoban
*__My Very First Mother Goose,__ edited by Iona Opie

Vinyl and Board Books for Babies and Toddlers

Choose books with round corners and clear pictures of familiar things to know, name, and talk about. For the littlest reader, single images on a page are easier to "read." There may be one word or no words on the page, but you can use many words as you talk about the familiar bojects and relate them to baby. Older babies will like pointing and finding the red cup that's full of milk or the sweet yellow banana. Little stories that center on the child's world are most appropriate for young toddlers. Here are some favorites.

Vinyl

■ Bath Books

(FunFax/DK $4.95) Smooth edges, soft tubbable vinyl, and clear pictures make this a safe, interesting bet for early book tasters and page turners. Titles include: **Colors, Sea Animals,** and **1,2,3.** 6 mos. & up.

■ Spot's Toys

(by Eric Hill, Putnam $3.95) The famous pooch (you'll be getting to know him in many toddler books) is introduced in this vinyl book with all his toys.

■ Scrub-A-Dub-Dub

(by Joanne Barkan/illus. by Sharon Holm, Random House $4.99) Baby testers loved the "magic" of this vinyl book with illustrations that change color when they hit water. Told in simple rhyme. Also: **Splish! Splash!** 8–24 mos.

Board Books

■ Baby's Animal Friends

(by Phoebe Dunn, Random House $3.95) Clear photos of real animals with children, two subjects babies love to watch. Fits in a fat little fist. Also **Farm Animal** and **Zoo Animals.**

■ Baby Animals—Black and White

(by Phyllis Limbacher Tildes, Charlesbridge $4.95) Bold black-and-white faces of a panda, seal, bunny, puppy, kitten and other animals make for interesting looking for babies. 6 mos. & up.

■ **Baby Faces Smile!**

(by Roberta G. Intrater, Scholastic $4.95) Babies love looking at babies and faces, and this charming board book has photos of multi-ethnic babies with a simple little rhyme that reflects what grown-ups always say when they take photos. 6 mos. & up.

■ **Baby's First Words**

(photos by Lars Wik, Random $2.95) A little book that fits easily in tiny hands, with photos of familiar things.

■ **I See** and **I Touch**

(by Rachel Isadora, Greenwillow $6.95 each) Two classic baby books trace baby's day and the things he sees and touches.

■ **Old MacDonald** and **The Itsy-Bitsy Spider**

(by Rosemary Wells, Scholastic $4.95) Now you can sing a book to your baby instead of just reading with this new series of familiar songs done in sturdy board books. As always, Wells's illustrations are scrumptious! PLATINUM AWARD '99. Also, **The Bear Went Over the Mountain.** 2 & up.

■ **Pat-A-Cake**

(by Tony Kenyon, Candlewick $3.99) Lively illustrations with the traditional rhyme capture child and baker patting up a perfect cake that's marked with a B for baby and me. 1 & up.

■ **Peek-A-Boo!**

(by Jan Ormerod, Dutton $6.99) Lift the flaps on this cardboard book to reveal all sorts of babies playing peek-a-boo. Just right for early lap games. 1 & up.

■ **Show Me!**

(by Tom Tracy/illus. by Darcia Labrosse, HarperCollins $5.95) Knowing and naming your nose, chin, tummy, etc. is fun for toddlers and this little rhyme will work well for such games. 1 & up.

■ **What Is It?**

(by Tana Hoban, Greenwillow $4.95) Striking photos of objects baby will recognize, by a master photographer.

Resources for Parents

■ Lullabies

(Metropolitan Museum/Harcourt Brace $23) Words and music for 35 memorable lullabies are illustrated with works of art from the Met's collection. PLATINUM AWARD '98. Also: **A Child's Book of Lullabies** with paintings by Mary Cassatt (DK $12.95) Either makes a glorious gift for new parents.

■ My First Songs

(illus. by Jane Manning, HarperCollins $9.95) If you can't remember all the words to most of the nursery songs you sort of know—here's a picture book for you. It includes "Wheels on the Bus," "Eensie Weensie Spider," and many other oldies but goodies. Also: **My First Nursery Rhymes.** 1 & up.

■ My Very First Mother Goose Boardbooks

(edited by Iona Opie/illus. by Rosemary Wells, Candlewick $8 each) Wells's art adds a deliciously witty view that makes these old rhymes new again. "Wee Willie Winkie" and "Little Boy Blue" are the best of the lot. You'll use them as a resource for rhymes to recite aloud long before you sit and read them to your child. PLATINUM AWARD '98.

■ Pat-a-Cake and Other Play Rhymes

(by Joanna Cole and Stephanie Calmenson, Morrow $14) Thirty hand-clapping and knee-bouncing rhymes to say and play almost any time of day each with "how-to" drawings.

■ Baby Story

(Chimeric $29.95) Create your own story about your baby with favorite photos and captions. Decorate the pages with over 100 Mrs. Grossman's stickers, choose the cover color and the book will be returned professionally typeset and bound. Kit price includes one copy, but of course you can order additional copies for the grandparents! A great shower present. (800) 706-8697.

SMART PARENT TRICK

Babies and toddlers love crumpling, ripping, and tasting newspapers and magazines, but the printing ink can be dangerous to ingest. Let them eat cake—not ink!

Older Toddlers

Toddlers are ready for new kinds of books. Just as they can understand almost anything you say, they can also follow books with small stories that center on their familiar world.

They like playful language with rhythm, rhyme, and repetitive lines they can chime in on. They enjoy stories about children like themselves, and playful animal stories in which a dog or a bear is really a "child in fur." Toddlers also love books about real things like colors, caterpillars, and cars. Choose books you really like, because toddlers like to hear their favorites again and again!

TEN BLUE CHIP BOOKS EVERY TODDLER SHOULD KNOW

* **Goodnight Moon,** by Margaret Wise Brown
* **Jamberry,** by Bruce Degen
* **Wheels on the Bus,** adapted by Paul Zelinsky
* **Polar Bear, Polar Bear, What Do You Hear? & Brown Bear, Brown Bear, What Do You See?** by Bill Martin Jr.
* **Sheep in a Jeep,** by Nancy Shaw
* **Where's Spot?** by Eric Hill
* **The Little Red Hen,** by Byron Barton
* **You Go Away,** by Dorothy Corey
* **When You Were a Baby,** by Ann Jonas
* **The Very Hungry Caterpillar,** by Eric Carle

First Little Stories, Adventures & Mysteries

■ Big Dog and Little Dog Wearing Sweaters

(by Dav Pilkey, Harcourt Brace $4.95) Big and Little Dog are good friends who share small adventures in several small books. In this one, Little Dog has a sweater and he helps Big Dog find a sweater. 1 & up.

■ Hide-and-Seek Elmer

(by David McKee, Lothrop $11.95) Toddlers will enjoy this lift-the-flap adventure as Elmer seeks out his friend, Bird, who's hiding. A knowing and naming book for both animals and colors. 2 & up.

■ On My Own

(by Miela Ford, Greenwillow $5.95) Older toddlers will love the independent polar bear who likes to play. Ford's close-up photos of the roly-poly baby bear wiggling, stretching, climbing, and rolling are sure to please toddlers. A sturdy cardboard format for independent reading. 2½ & up.

■ Where Did Josie Go?

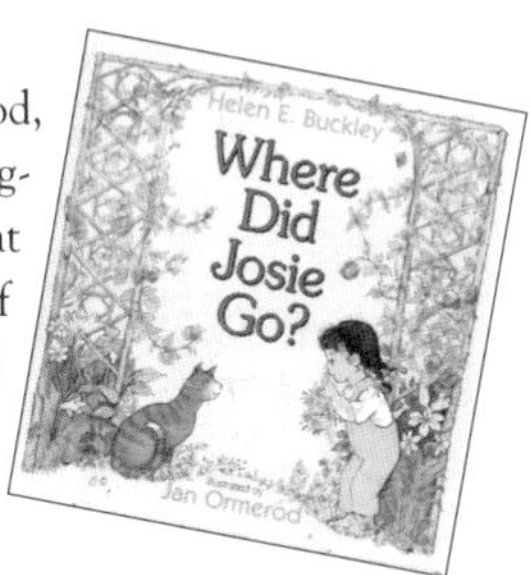

(by Helen E. Buckley/illus. by Jan Ormerod, Lothrop $16) Mommy (who is mightily pregnant), Daddy, brother, and the family cat and dog all join in on Josie's little game of hide and seek. Thoughout this tot-sized mystery young listeners will be able to discover Josie's feet. 2½ & up.

■ Peek-A-Boo!

(by Janet & Allan Ahlberg, Viking $6.99) A reissue of a gem now in a sturdy boardbook format. One, two, three... what does baby see? Cut-out peek holes reveal details of family life and the busy scenes baby sees as each page is turned. 2½ & up.

■ Peek-A-Moo

(by Bernard Most, Harcourt Brace $5.95) Do you see the cow? Again and again tots will have the fun of spotting the little cow and calling peek-a-moo! PLATINUM AWARD. 2 & up.

■ Where's Spot?

(by Eric Hill, Putnam $11.95) Spot the pup is missing! Where can he be? Lift the flaps and see! Not much story here, but the suspense is toddler-sized. Be prepared: Little hands may not be able to life without a rip. Series is uneven—some are better than others.

Rhythm & Rhyme & Repetitive Lines

■ Cows In the Kitchen

(by June Crebbin/illus. by Katherine McEwen, Candlewick $15.99) Using the rhythm of "Skip to My Lou," this bouncy nonsense song is illustrated with cows prancing in the kitchen, pigs munching in the pantry, and sheep bouncing on the sofa while Tom Farmer sleeps. PLATINUM AWARD '99.2 & up.

■ I Love You As Much

(by Laura K. Melmed/illus. by Henri Sorensen, Morrow $6.95) Each of the animal mothers in this lyrical lullaby tells its baby how much love she feels. Reissued in a board book edition. 1½ & up.

■ Jamberry

(by Bruce Degen, HarperCollins $3.95) A totally delicious nonsense rhyme about every kind of berry in the world. The playful lilt of the rhyme and rhythm will be enjoyed and chanted by preschoolers as well. 2 & up.

■ Sheep in a Shop BLUE CHIP

(by Nancy Shaw/ill. by Margot Apple, Houghton Mifflin $12.95) Five woolly sheep set out on a zany shopping trip. After stirring up a storm in a store, they end up getting fleeced to pay the bill. Tots love the bouncy rhyme and birthday cake ending! 2 & up.

■ Row, Row, Row Your Goat

(by Bernard Most, Harcourt Brace $5.95) A playful variation on "Row Your Boat" with a crew of critters that grows bigger with every turn of a page. PLATINUM AWARD '99. 1½ & up.

■ You're Just What I Need

(by Ruth Krauss/illus. by Julia Noonan, HarperCollins $14.95) A toddler hiding under a blanket plays a game with Mom who keeps guessing what might be under there. Toddlers will love all the "No. I'm not..." answers in the book and will want to play the game too. PLATINUM AWARD '99. 2 & up.

Slice-of-Life Books

■ Bath-Time Boots

(by Satoshi Kitamura, Farrar, Straus $4.95) Toddlers who like to dodge the tub will see the humor of this merry chase in which Boots the cat tries to avoid tub time and accidentally gets into the swim of it. 2 & up.

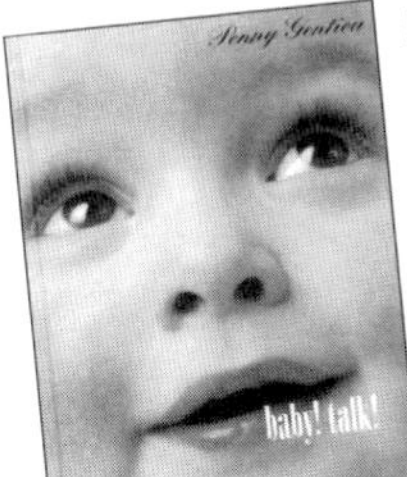

■ Baby! Talk!

(by Penny Gentieu, Crown $13) We're sure this big book with photos of babies playing patty-cake, peek-a-boo, and so big will make a hit with lap sitters. It will be even better when it's reissued in cardboard so little hands won't rip it! 1 & up.

■ I Love You Just the Way You Are

(by Virginia Miller, Candlewick $15.99) George reassures Bartholomew that he loves him even when he's having a rough day. A comforting book for both toddlers and their parents. PLATINUM AWARD '99. 2½ & up.

■ Max's New Suit

(by Rosemary Wells, Dial $5.99) Max is going to a party and his bossy sister is trying to teach him to dress himself. Ruby never learns! A reissue with bright new art in a boardbook. 2½ & up.

■ You and Me, Little Bear

(by Martin Waddell/illus. by Barbara Firth, Candlewick $15.99) Like so many children, Little Bear finds that Big Bear is busy doing Big Bear things like gathering wood, carrying water, and making things tidy. Little Bear helps and then finds things to do alone. Little Bears everywhere will relate to this tender tale that reflects their own hunger for time together. A new gem from a fine series that breaks the gender stereotype with male Big Bear caregiver. 2½ & up.

Coping With Life's Little Ups & Downs

■ Bunny Bungalow

(by Cynthia Rylant/illus. by Nancy Hayashi, Harcourt, Brace $14) Here's a honey of a bunny tale about moving to a new home. Told in sweet, easy couplets, this is just the right kind of reassurance young movers need. 2½ & up.

■ Just You and Me

(by Sam McBratney/illus. by Ivan Bates, Candlewick $15.99) It's about to storm, and Little Goosey is out with Big Gander Goose. As they look for shelter other creatures offer them cover but Little Goosey wants to be alone with Big Goose, who understands. 2½ & up.

■ My Own Big Bed

(by Anna G. Hines/illus. by Mary Watson, Greenwillow $15) A comforting book about making the transition from crib to bed. 2½ & up.

■ When Mama Comes Home Tonight

(by Eileen Spinelli/illus. by Jane Dyer, Simon & Schuster $14) With tender illustrations and lyrical rhymes, this celebrates day's end when Mama comes home. Working mamas and their tots will enjoy this again and again. PLATINUM AWARD '99. 2 & up.

Potty Corner (Results not Guaranteed!)

■ Going to the Potty

(by Fred Rogers/photos by Jim Judkis, Putnam $5.95) In his usual reassuring way, Mr. Rogers talks with children about using the potty. This photo essay reinforces the idea that using a potty is another step toward growing up. Also excellent: **Your New Potty,** by J. Cole, Morrow. 2 & up.

■ Koko Bear's New Potty

(by Vicki Lansky, Bantam $3.95) Koko is a little bear who is learning how to become more independent by using the potty. Each page also includes a few of Lansky's tips for parents on their role. 2 & up.

Sweet Dreams—Bedtime Books

■ Good Night, Baby Bear

(by Frank Asch, Harcourt Brace $14) Every child who has ever stalled about going to sleep will relate to Baby Bear who wants a snack, a drink, and even the moon. Mama Bear is not only patient—she even delivers the moon! A snuggle-up kind of bedtime tale. PLATINUM AWARD '99. 2–5.

■ Good Night Spot

(by Eric Hill, Putnam $3.99) In just a few sturdy cardboard pages Spot gets tired, takes his bath, gets ready for bed and goes to sleep. If only a toddler's life were that simple! 1 & up.

■ Goodnight Moon

(by Margaret Wise Brown/illus. by Clement Hurd, HarperCollins $6.95) Happy news! This bedtime classic is available in a sturdy board book that toddlers can enjoy without ripping. 18 mos. & up.

■ Guess How Much I Love You

(by Sam McBratney/illus. by Anita Jeram, Candlewick $6.99) When Big Nutbrown Hare puts Little Nutbrown Hare to sleep, they get into an insoluble game of measuring their love for each other. Breaks the usual gender agenda of moms tucking little ones in and is newly issued in a sturdy board book. PLATINUM AWARD '97. 2 & up.

Early Concept Books— Color, Counting and More

■ Big and Little

(by Margaret Miller, Greenwillow $15) Toddlers, pleased with how big they've gotten, will be delighted with this collection of photos showing kids doing "big" things like pulling a wagon, playing with blocks, and having pretend tea. 2½ & up.

■ Boats; Planes; Trains; Trucks

(by Byron Barton, HarperCollins $2.95 each) These popular cardboard books have been upsized this year with the same bold graphics that introduce the ups, downs, ins, and outs of each form of transportation. 1–4.

■ **Do Monkeys Tweet?**

(by Melanie Walsh, Houghton Mifflin $15) Do dogs oink? Do horses bark? Older toddlers will giggle smugly at the totally ridiculous questions and gloat at how smart they are because they know the name of the animal that tweets, cheeps, barks, oinks, or... whatever, on the turn page. From the author of **Do Pigs Have Stripes?** 2½ & up.

■ **Freight Train**

(by Donald Crews, Greenwillow $16) An utterly Spartan text runs through this Caldecott Honor book that young train buffs can also learn their colors by. 2 & up.

■ **The Happy Book**

(by Diane Muldrow/illus. by Patti Ann Harris, Scholastic $13.95) With lots of textures to feel, flaps to lift, scratch-and-sniff scents to smell—this is an ideal touchy-feely book about feeling. Unlike many, this one is solid enough to handle without fear of parts being pulled off and chewed! 2 & up.

■ **Here Are My Hands**

(by Bill Martin Jr. & John Archambault/illus. by Ted Rand, Holt $6.95) With utter simplicity the rhymes in this sturdy board book name parts of the body and what they do. Features a multicultural cast of children from all over the world. 2 & up.

■ **I Spy Little Numbers**

(by Jean Marzollo/illus. by Walter Wick, Scholastic $6.99) Older toddlers will love naming the objects in the riddles on the left page and finding them embedded in the more complex picture on the right. There are several of these sturdy cardboard books adapted from the series designed for older kids. This one has numerals and some counting in it. Also, **I Spy Little Wheels.** 2½ & up.

■ **Let's Go Visiting**

(by Sue Williams/illus. by Julie Vivas, Harcourt Brace $15) A boy and his dog go visiting the colorful animals on a farm. This big color and counting (from 1–6) book has a repetitive refrain that toddlers will soon recite as the pages are turned.

■ Little Buddy Goes Shopping

(by Patrick Yee, Viking $10.95) A jaunty bunny goes shopping in this lift-and-look flap book. "Do you sell carrots?" he asks each shopkeeper. Young readers will soon read the windows of the shop and predict what's inside. 2 & up.

■ The Little Red Hen

(illus. by Byron Bargon, HarperCollins $6.95) Who will help the Little Red Hen do her work? Tots, who naturally love saying no, cheerfully chime in on the "Not I" refrain. A favorite reissued in a sturdy board book to read again and again. 2 & up.

■ Maisy at the Farm

(by Lucy Cousins, Candlewick $12.99) Every toddler's favorite mouse, Maisy is off to the farm, feeding the lambs, driving the tractor, gathering eggs. Lift the flaps and pull the tabs for peek-a-boo actions. Also new: **Happy Birthday, Maisy.** 2 & up.

■ Mary Wore Her Red Dress

(adapted by Merle Peek, Clarion $5.95) Kids love to make up their own verses for this old folk song that reinforces color concepts and clothing names. 2 & up.

■ Polar Bear, Polar Bear, What Do You Hear?

(by Bill Martin, Jr./illus. by Eric Carle, Henry Holt $13.95) Eric Carle's bold and brilliant beasts and Martin's simple but rhythmic rhyme make perfect harmony! Young listeners love chiming in on the telling. Also see **Brown Bear, Brown Bear, What Do You See?** 2 & up.

■ Ten

(by Keith Haring, Hyperion $6.95) Older toddlers who are into counting will have fun with counting the colorful Haring figures in this handsome board book. 2½–5.

■ Touch & Feel Farm

(DK $6.95) Tots can feel interesting textures of the animals pictured in this sturdy cardboard book. Also top-rated: **Wild Animals** and **Home** in the same series, but **Clothes** has a fuzzy feather that sheds. 1 & up.

■ **Trucks Trucks Trucks**

(by Peter Sís, Greenwillow $14.95) Sís uses a single action word and wonderfully bold drawings of a child driving a truck that's plowing or digging or doing what trucks do. 2½ & up.

■ **A Very Hungry Caterpillar**

(by Eric Carle, Philomel $15.95) Toddlers love the repetition of the text, the subject of eating, and poking their little fingers into all the little holes the hungry caterpillar has eaten through. A science book that will also be enjoyed by preschoolers. 2 & up.

■ **What Can You Do in the Rain?**

(by Anna G. Hines/illus. by Thea Kliros, Greenwillow $5.95) This and **What Can You Do in the Snow?** capture the typical things toddlers can begin to note and do in terms of the weather-which is often surprisingly fascinating to young children. Adorable multi-ethnic children. Sturdy cardboard format. 2 & up.

■ **Where's My Baby?**

(by H. A. Rey $4.95) We are delighted to welcome this reissued classic series of fold-out books, published decades ago, that have lost none of their appeal. Redone on sturdier stock for "read it again" requests. Also top-rated: **Anybody at Home?, See the Circus**, & **Feed the Animals.** 2 & up.

SMART PARENT TRICK

The more the TV is on, the more toddlers will watch. yet tots learn best from active doing rather than passive watching. Limit their viewing time and watch with them so that you can talk about and clarify what they see. There are lots of baby videos out there, but looking in a mirror would have more value than just watching other babies play. If you want a video for tots, make one with your toddler and familiar family members. With TV and videos, less is more!

III • Audio: Great Music

Music Exploration. Audio tapes and CDs are a great way to introduce children to a broad range of music, folksongs, marches, classics, and show tunes that they might not hear on the radio. These musical explorations are opportunities for dancing, conducting, drawing by, and even daydreaming.

Criteria. In testing new products, we continue to reject "children's music" that is preachy, overproduced, and, in many cases, condescending to young listeners. Our ultimate test is still whether we can stand being in a car with it or whether someone in the driver's seat or car seat screams, "Turn it off!"

Shopping Tips. We also recommend that you share your favorite music, whether it be contemporary, folk, jazz, classical, or show tunes. If you're enjoying the music, chances are it will be contagious.

We have listed the prices for tapes first and then for CDs, if available. Large music stores carry major companies like Disney, CBS, Sony Wonder, etc. We have provided numbers to help you locate titles from smaller recording companies that sell directly or through catalogs.

Music

Lullabies and Songs for the Very Young

■ A Child's Celebration of Lullaby

(Music for Little People $9.98/$12.98) What an eclectic mix of artists to sing you to sleep: Lena Horne, Raffi, Jerry Garcia, Kathie Lee Gifford, and Linda Ronstadt. First rate! (800) 409-2457.

■ At Quiet O'Clock

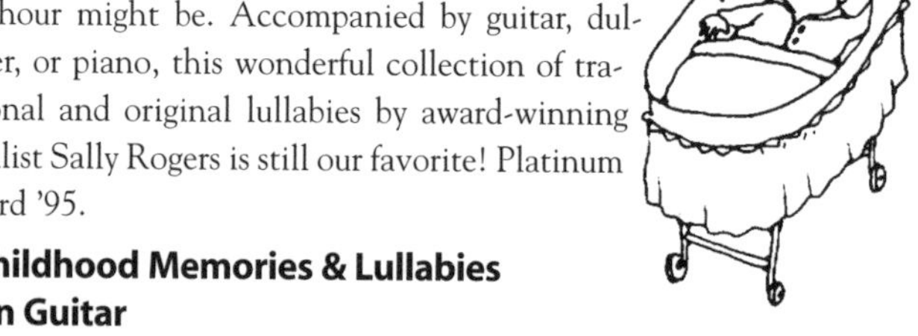

(Sally Rogers, Alcazar/Round River $8.98) These lullabies are just the ticket for a quiet time—whatever the hour might be. Accompanied by guitar, dulcimer, or piano, this wonderful collection of traditional and original lullabies by award-winning vocalist Sally Rogers is still our favorite! Platinum Award '95.

■ Childhood Memories & Lullabies On Guitar

(Michael Kolmstetter, Kolmstetter Musik $9.98/$14.98) You'll know these songs and be able to sing along to Kolmstetter's wonderful classical guitar recordings of familiar lullabies and nursery songs such as "Kum Ba Ya" and "Hush, Little Baby." Platinum Award '97 (800) 536-8409.

■ 40 Winks

(Jessica Harper, Alacazam! $9.98) After a long day of reviewing, Jessica Harper's latest recording was a welcome treat! This lyrical, jazzy, and soothing collection of original songs by Ms. Harper is the perfect kind of bedtime music for all. Platinum Award '99.

■ Nature Sounds

(Twin Sisters $8.99/$12.99) Soothing musical arrangements are accompanied with sounds of nature, e.g., rain, sea, a mother's heartbeat, and birds. Another option for sleepytime. (800) 248-8946.

■ Night-Night Lullabies

(The Dream Factory, Baby Boom Music $9.98) Testers young and old were ready for a nap with this calming collection of original and traditional lullabies.

■ Goodnight Guitar

(Ray Penny, Applewild Recordings $10.98/$14.98) Blues musician Ray Penny's collection of multicultural lullabies including such standards as "Brahms' Lullaby, " "Rock-a-bye," "Kumbaya," and "Raisins and Almonds" will do the trick for setting the mood for bedtime. Platinum Award '98. (888) 88-APPLE.

■ The Sun Upon the Lake is Low

(Mae Robertson & Don Jackson, Lyric Partners $10/$16) A sequel to Platinum '96 All Through the Night, this is a collection of glorious traditional and contemporary folk songs—a soothing way to end any day. Includes, among others, "Circle Game," "Michael Row Your Boat Ashore," and "Gaelic Lullaby." Platinum Award '98. (800) 985-8894.

■ Moondreamer

(Redwing $9.98/$15.98) Grab your blankie and get set for beautiful moondreams as Priscilla Herdman blends new and traditional lullabies and works her special silken magic. (800) 342-0295.

Music for Moving, Singing, & Dancing

■ Big Blues

(Kid Rhino $9.98/$15) Imagine a collection that includes B. B. King, Taj Mahal, Buckwheat Zydeco, and Maria Muldaur, among others. With classics as well as some new songs, might be called Blues 101. Parents will enjoy this one, too.

■ Birthday Songs

(Disney $9.98/$15.98) If you have no memory of the basic childhood musical games you played, such as "Hokey Pokey," "London Bridge," "Head, Shoulders, Knees and Toes," this is a must for your first preschooler's birthday party.

■ Elmopalooza

(Sony $9.95/$13.95) To celebrate 30 years of Sesame Street, Elmo and the gang are joined by such artists as Gloria Estefan, Jon Stewart, The Fugees, Rosie O'Donnell, and Kenny Loggins. If your family is in this zone, this will be a hit. We prefer this audio version to the video of the same name. PLATINUM AWARD '99.

■ Friends Forever

(Disney $9.95/$15.95) This is a surprisingly solid and musical recording about friendship that features Pooh and friends. While some songs are sung by the characters (Pooh's rendition of "You've Got A Friend" is interesting!), most are performed by artists and represent a rich mix of Cajun, Irish, and folk music. PLATINUM AWARD '99.

■ Raffi: The Singable Songs Collection

(Rounder $20/$30) Not one, not two, but three CDs—"Singable Songs for the Very Young"; "More Singable Songs"; & "Corner Grocery Store" include more than 50 top Raffi hits. Put this in your car for enough Raffi to get young travelers there and back. PLATINUM AWARD '98. (800) 443-4727.

■ Run, Jump, Skip and Sing

(Barney, Lyrick Studios $14.95) A very Barney collection of 25 songs for singing and moving to that will be a hit with true Barney fans. Includes now Barney standards: "Boom Boom, Ain't It Great To Be Crazy," and "I Love You." Be forewarned: the older "I hate Barney" testers needed to retreat to another room. 2 & up.

■ Kid'n Together: Singin' at the Swing Set

(Alex & Ben Meisel/Kid'n Together $9.98/$14.98) We loved the vitality of this recording that includes both upbeat toe-tapping tunes as well as sweet lullabies. Solid concepts, like shapes, rhyming, and please and thank you are reinforced without being teachy or preachy. A product of what seems to be the entire Meisel family—Alex & Ben provide the main vocals with their whole family getting into the act. (Of course, we look kindly on family ventures!). PLATINUM AWARD '99. (800) 543-6386.

■ Shakin' A Tailfeather

(Taj Majal et al., Music for Little People $8.98/$15.98) Intended to get the family up and dancing, here's a collection of classic dance tunes performed by renowned blues artists Taj Majal, Linda Tillery & the Cultural Heritage Choir, and Eric Bibb. Includes "Willie and the Hand Jive," "Oh Mary Mack," "The Name Game," and "Loop De Loop." Inspired by Ms. Tillery's early love of clapping and circle games. (800) 409-2457.

■ Songs From a Parent to a Child

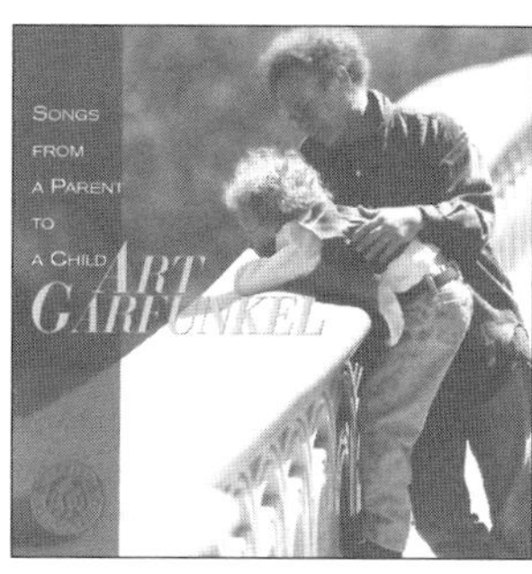

(Art Garfunkel, Sony $9.95/$13.95) Fans of Art Garfunkel will love this collection of songs including James Taylor's "Secret O' Life," The Beatles' "I Will," as well as traditional songs like "Now I Lay Me Down to Sleep." PLATINUM AWARD '99.

■ Sounds Familiar

(David Alpert, D&A Records $12/$18) The clarity of his voice as well as the use of the banjo, mandolin, guitar, harmonica, and dulcimer give Alpert's collection of original songs a rich, textured sound that makes you think of being on a porch with a gentle summer breeze. One of the best children's reçordings we've heard in years. Everyone in the car loved this one! PLATINUM AWARD '99. (203) 457-0855.

■ Swingin' in the Rain

(Maria Muldaur, Music for Little People $9.98/$15.98) Swing is back in vogue and this collection of tunes is fun for whole family. Songs include: "Aba Daba Honeymoon," "Zip-A-Dee-Doo-Dah," "A Bushel and A Peck," "Jeepers Creepers," and "A, You're Adorable." The almost title song is our least favorite—maybe because we can't separate the song from Gene Kelly. Our resident grandma knew all the words—to the amazement of her grandchildren.

■ Teaching Hippopotami to Fly

(CanTOO $19.95/$15.95) When we talk about what makes a winning children's audio, this is how it sounds! Real music and witty lyrics, all harmoniously blended by the Chenille Sisters. Platinum Award '98. (800) 830-1919.

Also recommended

Joanie Bartels' Adventures with Family and Friends (Youngheart Music $10.98/$13.98) 4 & up. Platinum Award '98. (800) 444-4287.
Timeless (Cathy Block, Intuition Music $9.98/$15.98) (800) 842-

SONG. **Goin' to the Zoo** (Tom Paxton, Rounder $9.50/$15) (800) 443-4727; **Hello Everybody!** (Rachel Buchman, A Gentle Wind $8.95) (888) 386-7664. **Little Voices in My Head** (Sing With Me $10/$14) (312) 271-5568. **Jump Up and Sing: Binyah's Favorite Songs** (Sony $9.98/$13.98).

Folk Tunes for All Ages

■ Bill Staines' One More River

(Red House Records $8.98/$17.98) If you are a folk music person, you'll need no introduction to Bill Staines. This isn't a collection of cutesie songs chosen for the kiddies. It's honest-to-goodness music—some somber, some classic, some less familiar, and all joyful. Accompanied by everything from banjoes to violins, congas to penny whistles, guitars to bass.

■ Ella Jenkins' Songs Children Love to Sing: A 40th Anniversary Collection

(Smithsonian Folkways $9.50) What a treat! Ella Jenkins, the ultimate songsmith for the young, has selected 17 of her favorite songs that she recorded during the last forty years, including "Miss Mary Mack" and "This Old Man." These are classic folksongs with plenty of repetition and easy sing, clap, and tap-along fun.

■ Pete Seeger For Kids & Just Plain Folks

(Sony $8.98/$17.98) An interesting mix of Seeger's classics such as "Michael Row Your Boat Ashore," "This Land Is Your Land," "Put Your Finger in the Air," plus a good many less familiar folksongs, many originally released in the '60s. All ages. Also recommended, **Pete Seeger's Family Concert.**

■ Peter, Paul & Mary Around the Campfire

(Warner Bros. $13.95/$17.95) This double CD collection is a treat and includes such favorites as: "If I Had a Hammer," "Blowin' In The Wind," and "Puff, The Magic Dragon." Celebrating their 38th

year together, their music is truly multi-generational. PLATINUM AWARD '99.

■ This Land Is Your Land

(Rounder $9.50/$15) Introduce your kids to the music of Woody and Arlo Guthrie singing such classics as the title song, "So Long, It's Been Good to Know Yuh," and "Riding In My Car. " PLATINUM AWARD '98. (800) 443-4727.

■ Water Sign

(DKI Inc. $10/$15) An uplifting, thoughtful, and wonderful collection of new and old folk songs that makes great quiet-time listening, including the best mermaid song we've ever heard. (212) 721-9382.

Also recommended:

A Child's Celebration of Folk Music (Music for Little People $9.98/$12.98) Platinum Award '97. (800) 346-4445; **Doc Watson Sings Songs For Little Pickers** (Alacazar $8.98/$11.98).

Multicultural Music

■ Cada Niño

(Tish Hinojosa, Rounder Records $11.95) A rare truly bilingual recording that celebrates Latino and American cultures with 11 songs sung in both English and Spanish. (800) 443-4727.

■ Canta Conmigo Vol. 2

(Senda Productions $12/$17) Educator and singer Juanita Newland-Ulloa blends folktales, dances, lullabies, and games into a new collection of lively Latin American songs for children learning Spanish and/or English. (510) 632-6296.

■ Cajun for Kids

(Papillion, Music for Little People $9.98/$15.98) Papillion, a Cajun musician, blends music and story in this get-up-and-move collection of Cajun music that includes such songs as "Down On the Bayou," "Jambalaya," and "You are My Sunshine." We could have done with less talking and even more music.

■ More Reggae For Kids

(RAS $11/$15) Get up and move to this collection of Reggae music that includes such variations as "Raindrops Keep Falling On My

Dread" and "Rasta Row the Boat Ashore." Performed by well-known Jamaican artists. (301) 588-5135.

■ Jumpin' Jack

(Jack Grunsky, BMG $8.98/$14.98) A wonderfully interesting mix of French, Spanish, English, Rajasthani, and Caribbean music. Songs include "Iko Iko" and "Songbirds." A treat!

■ Le Hoogie Boogie: Louisiana French Music for Children

(Michael "Beausoleil" Doucet et al., Rounder $9.98/$11.98) Looking for something different that will brighten everyone's spirits? Try a musical tour of Cajun country that will be sure to make you get up and dance. Wonderful! (800) 443-4727.

Music from Broadway and Hollywood

■ A Child's Celebration of Show Tunes

(Music For Little People $9.98/$12.98) A wonderful intro to some of the best-known show tunes from "Oliver!," "The Sound of Music," "The King and I," "Peter Pan," and "Fiddler on the Roof," with the added bonus of having them sung by the original casts. A real treat! (800) 346-4445.

■ The Lion King: Original Broadway Cast Recording

(Disney $9.98/$15.98) We get goose bumps every time we listen to the opening number. The Elton John and Tim Rice score is rich and magical! Short of a ticket to the hottest show on Broadway, bring this home for the whole family. PLATINUM AWARD '99.

■ Mary Poppins / Lion King / Aladdin / Beauty and the Beast / Pocahontas / Hunchback of Notre Dame / Mulan

(Disney $9.98/$15.98) Our testers loved listening to the scores from Disney's latest run of mega box-office hits. Disney enthusiasts will also want to consider **The Music of Disney** ($35.98/$49.98), a three-part set of 78 classic Disney tunes dating back to 1928.

■ My Little Broadway

(Sony $6.98/$9.98) Twelve well-known songs from Broadway hits performed by such artists as Mary Martin, Dick Van Dyke, Julie Andrews, and Andrea McArdle.

■ Peter Pan BLUE CHIP

(Mary Martin et al., RCA $9.95/$17) This is the original cast from the 1954 Broadway production and simply the best! No one sings "Never-Never Land" like Mary Martin!

Introducing the Classics

■ Bernstein Favorites BLUE CHIP

(Sony $7.98/$14.98) Children's classics "The Carnival of the Animals," "The Young Person's Guide to the Orchestra," and "Peter and the Wolf" are all part of this wonderful introduction to classical music.

■ Hush

(Yo-Yo Ma & Bobby McFerrin, CBS $9.98/$17.98) Our testers enjoyed the musical union of this world-renowned cellist and contemporary vocalist. Pieces range in style from "The Flight of the Bumblebee" to "Hoedown."

■ Kids Classics Series

(EMI $7.99/$10.99 each) Truly a hit-parade of classical music. On **Animals** you'll hear "The Carnival of the Animals," Itzhak Perlman narrating "Peter and the Wolf," and "The Flight of the Bumble-Bee." **Nature** includes Vivaldi's "Winter," Beethoven's "Pastoral Symphony," and Debussy's "Gardens in the Rain." Also recommended, **Toys, Lullabies.** Platinum Award '98.

■ The Mozart Effect, Vols.1–3

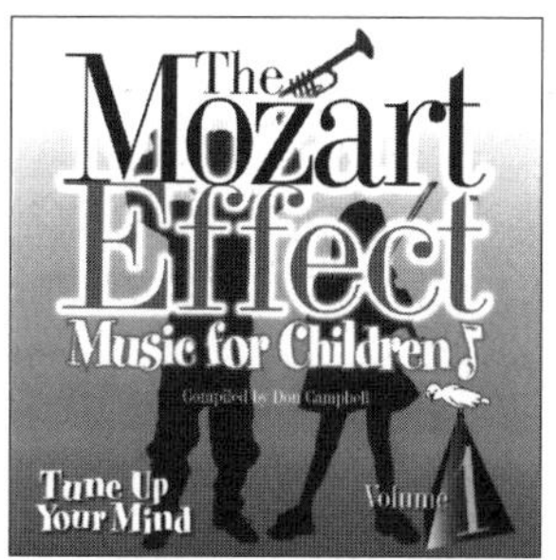

(BMG $8.98/$17.95) Responding to research that links the value of Mozart's music to learning, these three volumes offer a range of music performed by first class artists: **Vol. 1, Tune Up Your Mind; Vol. 2, Relax, Daydream & Draw;** and **Vol. 3, Mozart in Motion.** It couldn't hurt! PLATINUM AWARD '99. All ages.

■ The Power of Classical Music

(Twin Sisters $8.99/12.99) Music by Bach, Mozart, Schumann, and Grieg played by a 16 piece string ensemble. Beautiful arrangements are ideal for movement and dance time or for daydreaming. All ages. (800) 248-8946.

Resources

Catalogs

- **Family Planet Music** (800) 985-8894.
- **Music for Little People** (800) 409-2457. This great catalog is back in business with a wide selection of music, videos, and instruments.

Online

- **amazon.com**
- **cdnow.com**
- **cdworld.com**
- **etoys.com**
- **musicblvd.com**

Toys by Age & Stage

FIRST 6 MONTHS – MOSTLY HORIZONTAL

Gazing toys	Musical mobile* **remove by 5 months* Musical pull toy Crib mirror
Tracking toys	Soft rattles with patterns & sound
What they learn:	**Visual and auditory stimulation & tracking**
Grasping toys	Soft rattles with soft sounds
What they learn:	**Motivating baby to reach out & take hold of things**

6-12 MONTHS – VERTICAL

Manipulatives	Rattles and teethers with motion, sound, and varied textures, hand-held mirrors, crib activity center
First stacking toys	Fabric blocks
Filling & spilling toys	Containers with multiple pieces to taste, toss, and spill, e.g., baby blocks, giant beads
First bath toys	Simple floating balls, boats, ducks

Huggables	Soft doll, animals with easy-to-grasp limbs, stitched features
What they learn	**Developing eye-hand cordination, investigating through the senses, making things happen, two-handed play, refining use of fingers, discoveries in cause & effect**
First rolling toys	Soft fabric ball, for crawlers Chunky vehicles
What they learn	**Social games, active physical play**
Books	Cloth & cardboard books with familiar objects to know and name
What they learn	**Language and recognizing pictorial symbols of real objects**

1–2 YEARS – NEW MOBILILTY

First walking toys	Push toys for beginners, pull toys for steady walkers
First ride-on toys	Straddle wheeled toy (no pedals), low-to-the-ground rocking toys
First climbers	Low-to-the-ground climber with slide

What they learn:	**Toys that match new mobility, big muscles development, active play, imagination/early pretend**
Manipulatives	Toys with action and re-action, pop-ups, fill and dump, hammer toy
Blocks	Chunky plastic blocks, big card-board blocks
Bath toys	Floaters with multiple pieces that fit together, beakers for filling and spilling, tubbable doll
Art supplies	Big crayons and paper
What they learn	**Making more complex things happen, refining eye hand coordination, fine motor skills, problem solving, sit down play, non-verbal creative expression**
Early pretend toys	Phone, broom, garden tools, big trucks & cars
Huggables	Big enough to lug and hug or small enough to clutch and carry
Books	Sturdy books for little readers to handle, books with familiar objects and simple stories
What they learn:	**Budding imagination, role play & language**

2-3 YEARS OLDER TODDLERS — MORE MOBILITY & COMMUNICATION

Wheeled toys	Pedal-free cars to ride in, small wagon for deliveries, (older twos may be ready for pedals)
Balls	Big soft balls for rolling and bouncing

Equipment with Long-Term Use:

Climbers	Low-to-the-ground climber with slide, tunnels
Outdoor toys	Sandbox, shovels & pails, sand mill, low-to-the-ground gentle sprinkler, wading pool, rake, shovel garden tools, toddler swing, low slide, bubbles
Table & chair	Basic gear for snacks, and art and puzzles
Playhouse	Enclosure where kids can play alone or with a friend
What they learn:	**Active physical play, big muscles development, social play**
Pretend toys	Miniature settings of farms, garages, houses with multiple pieces, play kitchen, chunky dishes & pots, simple dress-up clothes, phone, sweeper

Huggables	Soft animals, dolls
What they learn:	**Use of imagination, role playing**
Construction toys	Wooden & plastic blocks with props, scaled-to-size vehicles and animals.
First puzzles	Simple whole-piece puzzles, stacking & size-order toys, big beads to string, shape sorter
Art materials	Big crayons, washable markers, play dough, glue
Musical toys	Simple drum, piano, maracas, xylophone
Bath toys	Toys for filling and spilling games
Books	Knowing and naming plus small stories that reflect everyday experiences
What they learn:	**Imagination and language as well as size and spatial relationships, eye-hand coordination, dexterity, problem solving, early use of symbols—making one thing stand for another**

Baby-Proofing Your Home

If this is your first baby, chances are your house needs baby-proofing today! Although you may have just a babe-in-arms, in no time at all your baby will be reaching out and moving about and you'll want to make your home a safe place to play. One of the best ways to spot problems is to get on your hands and knees and see your home from a baby's eye view. You may need to put things away for this period of your child's life.

Safety Checklist

We've prepared a safety checklist that you may want to copy and share with relatives the baby will be visiting often.

For all rooms:

- ☐ Do not use old baby carriers, portable cribs, swings, safety gates, car seats without checking first for recalls. As tempting as it may be to use a hand-me-down, many juvenile products are recalled for safety problems. Check with the Consumer Product Safety Commission or the manufacturer before you reuse. (800) 638-2772.
- ☐ Install window guards above ground level. Loops on window blind cords can be a strangulation hazard. Cut the loops or buy safety attachments that keep cords out of reach.
- ☐ Place decals on glass doors at toddler level.
- ☐ Sharp corners of tables, counters, and even fireplace ledges need to be covered to protect from serious injuries.
- ☐ Secure bookcases, grandfather clocks, large televisions, and wall units that can topple over if climbed on or bumped into.

- ☐ Fireplaces need to be outfitted with safety screens.
- ☐ Check houseplants—many can make your child very sick and several are even poisonous.
- ☐ Be sure that kids do not have access to exercise machines. Each year children lose digits from playing with exercise bikes.
- ☐ Tablecloths and cords of lamps are easily pulled by crawling babies. Switch to placemats and tuck cords out of reach.
- ☐ Cover all open electrical outlets with special covers so baby can't poke objects into them.
- ☐ Remove your breakable treasures from coffee tables. Sure, baby needs to learn not to touch- but not during these early years. You want to make your home baby friendly.
- ☐ Make sure the VCR is out of reach. Toddlers are famous for trying to see how many different things can fit in the slot!
- ☐ Move cleansers and other supplies from under the sink or other reachable locations. Put safety locks on doors and drawers that hold supplies that could endanger curious tots.
- ☐ Remove tippable floor lamps that can fall on baby and/or start a fire. Place behind furniture where baby does not have access if necessary to keep in the house.
- ☐ Put all medicines out of reach and remember toddlers are great climbers. Even vitamins can pose a serious health hazard to young children, and many look like candy. Bedside tables and open shelves are not secure locales.

Nursery:

All the above, plus:

- ☐ Check crib to make sure it's up today's safety standards. Slats should be no more than 2⅜" apart.
- ☐ You should not be able to fit more than two fingers

between the mattress and the crib.

- ☐ Bumpers should be tied down securely in at least six locations. Crib toys should also be fastened down at both the top and the bottom.
- ☐ Before your baby can reach the mobile, raise or remove it!
- ☐ Be sure sheets fit securely around the mattress.
- ☐ Do not place stuffed animals, large pillows, or cushy quilts in the crib. Several issues at play: Experts suggest that to reduce the risk of SIDS there should be nothing in the crib that can trap carbon monoxide in. Stuffed animals also provide a dangerous stepping platform for up and over the railing.
- ☐ Do not use toy chests without safety latches. Open shelves for toys are actually safer and easier to organize and use.

Kitchen:

All the above, plus:

- ☐ Invest in cabinet locks and covers for stove dials.
- ☐ Remove all cutlery from drawers that little hands can reach up into without seeing what they're touching. A countertop knife holder is a safer bet for sharp knives.
- ☐ Never leave a pail with water in it unattended. Babies and toddlers have been known to fall in and drown.

Bathroom:

All of the above plus:

- ☐ Medicines need to be put out of reach in childproof containers.
- ☐ Add slip-resistant decals to bottom of tub.
- ☐ Add a surge protector to prevent accidental scalding.
- ☐ Place a cover over tub spout to prevent burning or bumped heads.

- ☐ Add a toilet seat latch to prevent accidental drowning.

Garage:

- ☐ Be sure that if you have an electric garage door that it is up to safety standards. Test with a small doll. How far does it go down before it goes back up?
- ☐ Be sure to keep your car doors locked and your keys with you.
- ☐ Paint, cleaning fluids, tools all need to be up out of harm's way.

Baby CPR

Taking a baby CPR class is a great idea for parents and care providers. You should also learn how to do the Heimlich maneuver on children. It is also not well known that the Heimlich maneuver can also be used to expel water from drowning victims. Accidental drowning in the home is one of the leading causes of death of children under the age of five.

Tell the Grandparents… How Things Have Changed

When you were a baby you almost certainly had a "Crib Gym" strung across the bars of your crib rail for batting at. Some had dangly bells, rings, and turning balls that a baby could easily activate. Unfortunately, too many gyms could also catch a sleeve or entrap a baby strong enough to try to pull up. In fact, more than a few babies died by being hung in crib gyms—especially those with stretchy elastic. These toys are no longer considered safe.

Gone, too, are the soft slouchy bounce chairs that all too many babies bounced and tipped over, and so are the walkers that propelled many babies into furniture and down steps. Old playpens, baby swings, gates for stairways, carseats, cribs, toy chests, and portable cribs have changed dramatically in the past decade.

The fact that you survived these toys and equipment is

not a good enough reason to pass them on. Consider them as outdated as the car your parents drove back when.

Chances are that most toys and equipment that may have been put away for safe keeping are totally unsafe! Even treasures like sterling silver and mother of pearl rattles from the past are often too small or have small parts that no longer pass today's safety standards. Similarly, beautiful old wooden painted toys were often painted with lead paint. Such sentimental keepsakes may be special to you, but are too dangerous for your child to use.

Top-Rated Mail-Order Catalogs & On-Line Sites

For busy families, mail-order catalogs and on-line services are a time-saving way to shop. This list includes companies that feature many of the products we recommend.

Children's Catalogs

These catalogs offer a variety of toys, puzzles, games and outdoor equipment. Some also have selected books, videos and audios.

Back to Basics Toys	**(800) 356-5360**
Constructive Playthings	**(800) 832-0572**
FAO Schwarz	**(800) 426-8097**
Gifts for Grandkids	**(888) 472-6354**
Grand River Toy Co.	**(800) 567-5600**
Grandparent's Toy Connection	**(800) 472-6312**
Hand in Hand	**(800) 872-9745**
HearthSong	**(800) 325-2502**
One Step Ahead	**(800) 274-8440**
Right Start Catalog	**(800) 548-8531**
Sensational Beginnings	**(800) 444-2147**

School Catalogs of Interest

Community Playthings	**(800) 777-4244**
Environments	**(800) 342-4453**

Specialty Catalogs

Chinaberry (books)	(800) 776-2242
Family Planet Music	(800) 985-8894
Lego Shop at Home	(860) 763-4011
Music for Little People	(800) 409-2457
T.C. Timber (wooden toys)	(800) 245-7622

On-Line Sites

amazon.com
barnesandnoble.com
brainplay.com
cdnow.com
cdworld.com
etoys.com
kidflix.com
musicblvd.com
redrocket.com

Subject Index

Brand Name and Title Index

NOTE: Toys and equipment are listed under manufacturer or distributor. The following codes are used for titles of works: (A) = Audio tape; (B) = Book; (M) = Magazine; (V) = Video.